WEALTH BY SOUL DESIGN

Leverage

Your Unique Inner Magic

For Wealth

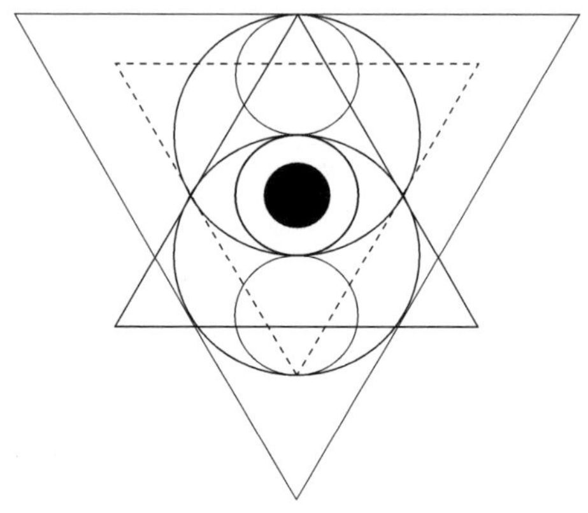

For Busy Coaches & Healers
on a Mission to Awaken Humanity

Wealth By Soul Design

Scale Your Business Into
Multi-6 or 7-Figure Empire
With The Badass
Conscious F.U.T.U.R.E. Method

BY EUGENIA OGANOVA

WEALTH BY SOUL DESIGN

Scale Your Business Into multi-6 Or 7-Figure Empire with The Badass Conscious F.U.T.U.R.E. Method.

This publication is designed to provide accurate and authoritative information regarding the subject matter covered. It is sold with the understanding that the publisher is not engaged in rendering legal, accounting, or other professional services. If you require legal advice or other expert assistance, you should seek the services of a competent professional.

Disclaimer: The author makes no guarantees of the results you'll achieve by reading this book. All business requires risk and hard work. The results and client case studies presented in this book represent results achieved working directly with the author. Your results may vary when undertaking any new business venture or marketing strategy.

Published by Pravda, Inc.

ISBN (paperback): 978-0-9793817-37
ISBN (eBook): 978-0-9793817-44

www.EugeniaOganova.com

CONTENTS

"Embrace thy unique inner Light and thy inherent Power, and thou shalt shine as a Star."

- AKHENATEN, THE PHARAOH OF EGYPT,
18TH DYNASTY, 1342 BC

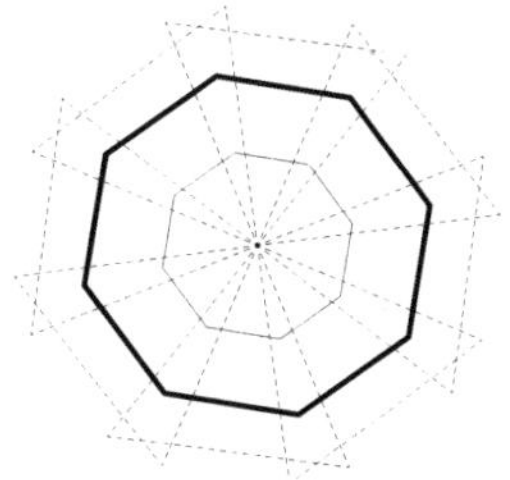

INTRODUCTION

Welcome, dear Leader! I'm so glad that you're here.

If you've picked up this book, I might guess the reasons.

One, you're probably a coach, healer, conscious expert, holistic professional, or teacher with a big Mission that you feel in your Soul you're meant to show up for. You're done playing small!

Two, you're probably not a total newbie. You have great results with paying clients and know your expertise, you've already created some success — maybe occasionally climbed to a $10k month and wish this was a regular occurrence, perhaps had a high 5-figure launch, maybe created six figures, even multi-6 figures in your service-based business.

Three, even though you're not driven by money alone, you desire to grow your coaching or healing business to multi 6 or even 7 figures, and you see yourself scaling sustainably, but you've tried cookie-cutter business systems and they didn't fit you for various reasons, so you're still looking…

Four, you are a busy woman, who is probably responsible for a lot (from your family, your business, your team if you have any, to your own inner navigation and success that results from your push forward). You are strong yet you know you cannot go on like this (or you might just burnout!) You are impatient, you're tired of walking in circles, and you want it all NOW.

Five, you want it YOUR way.

This book exists because I have seen too many amazing badass spiritually conscious female coaches and healers who have mind-blowing superpowers go over-worked with low-end client and remain underpaid because they just don't know that much about actually being a CEO of their business, and last but not the least, because this world needs us.

If we, conscious women who have insight, abilities, and powers that are not quite linear but so needed on this planet right now — if we don't show up — humanity is in for a confusing ride, riddled with manipulation and trauma.

The ones we were waiting for — to awaken humankind, to elevate consciousness, release ancestral baggage, to help people embody love, reconnect with abundance, and live in peace — we are them. We are the ones we were waiting for! But… if you are not well financially supported to do your amazing humanity-changing work in the world, you will burn out.

And I am here to change that for you.

This book is to help you see YOU in all your glory and unique badass magnificence,
- ❖ with lots of solid linear business strategies laid out
- ❖ and many nonlinear Quantum Creation strategies thrown in.

Another reason this book exists so that you'll walk away with everything you need to know to transform your low-end stressful coaching/healing hustle into a simplified high-ticket business
- ❖ that is aligned with your unique Soul Design Strategy
- ❖ and positioned to sustainably grow to multi-6 and 7-figures
- ❖ without having to work harder.

And then are inspired to work with me and my team to show you how to leap there faster and with more ease.

In this book I will help you see the parts of your business that are currently in your blind spot — so that you can clearly understand where you must put your efforts if you want to not only serve your clients at the highest level but do so in a sustainable and extremely profitable way. It's time to take your business seriously and quantum-leap into the level you and I both know you're meant to play at!

Then I will show you how the **Conscious F.U.T.U.R.E. Methodology** I've developed is specifically designed to get you there — to position your business (coaching, mentoring, healing) to sustainably grow into multi 6 and even 7 figures. This is the method I personally used to scale my business and became a self-made millionaire, and what I use with my clients to get them from an overworked place of so many one-off sessions clogging their schedule and charging around $100 per hour, to selling $5,000, $10,000, even $15,000 awesome Soul-aligned offers with ease.

Then we will dive into all the nitty-gritty details of the process, why traditional business techniques might not have worked for you before, what to watch out for in your offer creation and marketing, and how to adjust your trajectory to land in the place that so clearly resembles your Vision your head will spin!

And, of course, I won't leave you hanging — I'll show you how you can start to implement the information in this book right now.

The methodology you're about to discover has been my life, and applied to my business, has transformed it again and again. The benefits go beyond working with dream clients and getting paid handsomely, they extend onto the rest of my, and my clients, lives. I have faith that you'll be able to make the connection for yourself as well.

Throughout the book I'm sharing a ton of spiritual and business advice, and lessons I've learned from over twenty years of entrepreneurship, having made all the detours and business "mistakes", and yet still here, sustainably successful.

This book will give you many realizations and tools, but it's really a book about designing a vehicle to implement your Mission. You know you're here for a reason. You know you are meant for way bigger things that you are tinkering with right now. I will guide you toward a business strategy that brings you time-freedom and financial freedom while fully expressing your Soul purpose.

I believe we are all meant to be wealthy — that abundance is the base frequency of this Universe. But attracting wealth of clients, money, opportunities, takes dedication that most people choose not to put in.

If you are working with clients now and seeing awesome results and transformations in them, this is a clue that you also have a pre-installed-by-your-Soul means to attract wealth to be fully financially resourced! Why? Because this Universe is a very efficient place, and it will never put a glorious Soul Mission in your heart without giving you the tools to achieve it!

I want you, dear unique, hard-working, badass goddess on a Mission, to remember these 3 points — these are the mindset shifts that transformed my life from pressure-launching a new workshop every month, 12-hour days, and crunchy clients into a streamlined 7-figure empire with 3-day work week, soulmate clients, and sustained momentum:

Point #1: Your expertise and unique powers are needed in the world NOW — but the only way your business is sustainable is if it is aligned to your natural way and based on your Soul Design Strategy.

Point #2: The more you claim your Soul Expertise and show up in your badass unique magic, the more money you will make.

Point #3: The best method to find high-ticket clients who will pay you more than $5k for your Soul-aligned offers and sustainably grow to multi-6 or 7-figures without sacrificing your sanity, spiritual growth, or self-care-needs is laid out in this book. I call it The Conscious F.U.T.U.R.E. Method.

It's a great pleasure to share with you what I know. Applying each step in my Conscious F.U.T.U.R.E. Method that you're about to learn in these pages will open you up to the path of being able to:

❖ Activate certainty in your Mission so you never again wobble in how to explain "this magic thing you do" to others!
❖ Attract these $5k or $10k+ clients and dive deep with them using your amazing superpowers.

- ❖ Create $10k, $20k, $50k+ months applying your efforts strategically without over-giving, over-teaching, or over-stressing.
- ❖ Manifest these $100k+ launches and events by Quantum-leaping into your most Soul-aligned timeline.
- ❖ Experience Spaciousness paired with Momentum that makes your business feel so juicy.

I believe that you are the type of a badass person to dive in and then actually DO it.

And do it YOUR way.

If you read this book and decide you'd like help implementing its strategies as quickly as possible, please book a call to chat here: eugeniaoganova.com/start

Helping people like you to create coaching businesses that generate multi-6 and even 7-figure wealth by leveraging your unique badass superpowers *(that you might not even think of claiming yet!)* is exactly what we do every day.

We're here to help YOU too.

To your success, my dear unique Goddess that knows she's magical and awesome!

- Eugenia

Part 1:

The Wake-Up Call — Get Real About Your Business

"Success is not final, failure is not fatal: it is the courage to continue that counts."

- WINSTON CHURCHILL

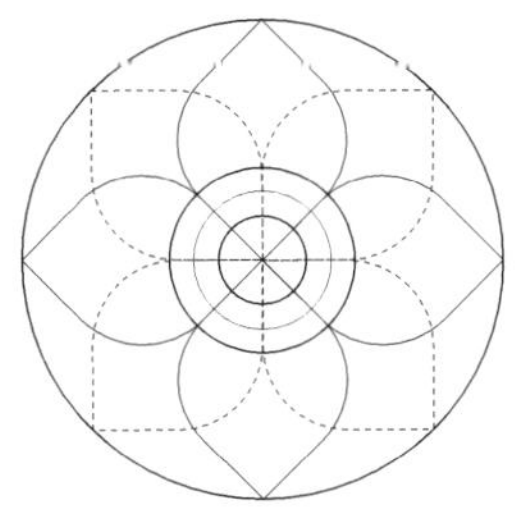

Chapter 1:

YOUR FUTURE POTENTIAL

Dear hard-working Leader of conscious transformation, let me share something with you that I know you're going to love! The methodology I'm about to reveal to you in this book is the result of my own struggle (cue the drama!) to find that elusive balance between being my authentic self (yep, I do it my way!) while still having plenty of time for my spiritual practice and serving my clients with aligned integrity. Oh, and did I mention generating some serious income too?

Later, I'll share with you the exact strategies I'm using to make that happen, but for now, consider this:

❖ Because of aligning my entire life with my Soul Design Strategy,
❖ And being able to clearly articulate the value of my Soul Expertise,
❖ My business is both simple and profitable.

As you're reading this book, today, I am able to work less than three days per week and generate over a million in revenue and help conscious women like you, in a Soul-led way that feels so freaking natural, without sacrificing time for spiritual needs or self-care. Using my Conscious F.U.T.U.R.E. Method:

- ❖ I don't need to launch a new offer every month. I don't even have to do live launches unless I feel like it — because I have a simple strategy.
- ❖ I don't have to beg or convince people to work with me — they come to the sales calls wanting to work with me already — because my methodology is clear.
- ❖ I don't need a large team because most tasks are automated.
- ❖ I don't feed 'freebie seekers' and 'tire kickers' — I only attract people who already know I am their coach and just need to clarify the details in order to sign up — because I market from my Soul Expertise.
- ❖ I spend less than 15 minutes per day marketing my business because my content is Soul-aligned (batch creativity) and automated.
- ❖ I provide an incredible amount of value (free and low-end courses) that supports people who cannot afford to jump into my high-ticket containers, while activating the ones who can, no effort is ever wasted.
- ❖ While the majority of coaches struggle on the sales calls, I love sales (and teach my clients how to love it!) and only attract leads that love my work already (which is a part of my methodology).
- ❖ My frequency is multidimensional and in the highest integrity, my standards are higher than most, I am in the top 1% of the coaching industry as a self-made millionaire woman, I never have to prove anything — I am who I am. It is obvious — just by my energetic presence (never mind the success track record for over 25 years!)

In short, my Conscious F.U.T.U.R.E. Method is a unique asset that allows me to help you in the most leveraged way.

Your business methodology is a marketing asset. It will allow you too to create ease, flow, and momentum in the most Soul-led way you can imagine!

My hope is that this book is the one thing you need to pick up to ignite your badass inner magic and catapult you into the frequency you see yourself living at already.

If you're anything like me, I am one impatient woman! You could call me "spiritually ambitious-impatient" because I can just see the future so clearly, feel the power of my Vision, and I want it all NOW! I'll charge forward with lightning speed in a direction that feels totally aligned, and yeah, sure, I'll create some seriously mind-blowing results along the way, but let's be real, I'll also come close to killing myself in the process!

I'm a contradiction of "wanting to plan it all out" and "be prepared" and yet jumping off the cliff because it is aligned, pushing myself to the brink while looking for the parachute (or my wings!) These two sides of me were not reconciled very well before my methodology was revealed to me — but I knew that there had to be a way to include it all, without sacrificing any part of me to achieve success — because I know that's where the real magic happens.

I bet you have your own inner contradiction: wanting to be "prepared" and "safe" *(studying systems, wanting to get it right, trying to track the details)*, while itching to fly with your Soul and create magic using your amazing superpowers! *(acting on what is aligned, following your inspiration, trusting your intuition)*.

So, if you're ready to embrace your own inner impatience and become the well paid badass visionary leader you know you're meant to be, strap in, 'cause we're about to take things to the next level!

***

If you and I were in a private video call together, sipping our tea and talking business growth, you might tell me that you are "willing to work hard" if you only knew the "right direction" to put your efforts in because you're already doing "all the things", yet feel stuck. And mainly that you have a huge Mission but can't imagine working THIS hard for years more to eventually get there.

Believe me, I get you.

The path to 7 figure coaching, healing, or expert Empire is not "easy" — it cannot be so by definition or everyone would be doing it!

But it can have *ease* and be way simpler and much faster than you currently believe. You're in the right place.

You see, dear badass conscious Leader, if you were to spy on my sales calls before people sign up, this is what you'd hear:

> *"What I do is so different, I have no idea how to speak about it so people want to buy… but I am very good at it, and clients have amazing results. I just want to know what to say so they want to work with me."*

> *"It's embarrassing, I help my clients clarify their purpose and manifest an authentic life, but I feel like I can't seem to get clear on how to make my Mission work. Why is it so hard?! I feel like I keep going in circles."*

> *"I am fully booked with $200 appointments and exhausted, I barely have the time for my family! I want to sell what is Soul-aligned and charge more. I created a course for $6000 but no matter what I do, I can't sell it."*

"It took me a year to create a $3k program, I had all the videos and sales page done professionally, I did this complex launch, paid someone to run ads to it — I spent over $15,000 on all of this but only sold enough to barely break even. I know something is missing, I should be further along by now, there's got to be a better way!"

"I have many sales calls coming in from Instagram but people are flaky, they all "have to think about it" or "can't afford it". I felt scared about the $5k price, so I lowered it but still had to convince them to buy. It doesn't feel aligned to use pressure tactics but how do I convert them?"

"I got to $150k selling my programs, I have funnels and I know how to sign clients, but I can't breathe because I work 24/7. I want to scale to $500k but how do I do that if there will be even more of what I can barely handle now?"

"For the past four years I've been booked, I got to $200k selling my program but I'm bored running it. I feel that I am aligned with a different client now but all the people on my sales calls are newbies. I can help them but I am sick of it. How do I find a better client?"

In short, all of them are saying that they want a way to grow and scale that fits THEM and they want to shortcut the journey by Quantum-leaping into it already!

Why does It Feel so Hard?

Maybe you can relate?

You might be very busy helping your clients but you're already at capacity, you've purchased a ton of courses that you've tried to implement and it either made your business even more complicated and hard, or you gave up on implementing because none of this felt aligned.

If you are successful now, it is probably because of lots of hard work and putting pressure on yourself to make it happen. You should be proud of your success! But… **this hustle is NOT scalable**. Once you reach your time and energy capacity, you are capped.

We both know that building a business in a conscious way is definitely not easy. And that most of the "traditional business and marketing strategies" might not fit spiritual rebels like us. This is the main reason why it feels SO HARD.

It is NOT the actions you are taking for your business.
It is the energy of friction that is wrapped around these actions.

Building your business to 6-figures takes a lot of work.
Remember being terrified but showing up anyway? Agonizing about what you can actually offer and why prospects should care? Creating your first sales copy, first opt-in page, sending first emails to your growing list, and trying to find your voice on social media? Having to figure out who these people are and what to say that makes them invest? None of this was easy, right?

If you were afraid of hard things, you wouldn't have started this entrepreneurial journey in the first place.

Scaling it into multi-6 and even 7-figures — even more work.
Brainstorming how to attract more clients, facing some difficult client situations, streamlining your delivery, live-launching and creating congruent marketing campaigns, checking email in the middle of the night because some links don't work, hiring a team, resisting micromanaging…

I am not one of these coaches who promises everything to be "just ease and flow" if you are vibrating in high frequency and commune with your energy guides daily.

Business is work.

But there is a difference between
- ❖ "working hard" and struggling, hustling, forcing yourself to do what you think you should…
- ❖ vs "conscious effort" in the form of aligned actions, clear decisions, correct strategy and a ton of personal transformation.

And that difference is FRICTION.

If you are anything like me, you LOVE to dive into the energetics and inner work, play in the multi-D Universe, and study new things. Now imagine pairing this with a practical business strategy that fits you like a glove. The Soul Design is that natural strategy that is pre-installed in you, and it takes care of any friction so you can DO what is necessary.

The Power of Frictionless Flow

Let's examine three possible examples of my clients. I'll call the first one Julie.

What I'm about to share is a common picture among my clients.

Julie came to us, as most of our clients do, feeling:
- ❖ Overworked;
- ❖ Stressed;
- ❖ Underpaid.

She is a gifted healer and mentor, but felt stuck in the drama of low-paying clients. She was selling $150 sessions and helping everyone who came along. Even though she felt so much love for her clients, she was on the edge of a burnout, responding to clients at all hours, dealing with so much client crisis. She felt she was meant to help her clients on a way deeper level than she was, but she couldn't fit more depth into her one-hour sessions. She was exhausted.

Utilizing the methodology you're going to read more about in this book, it became clear that she was correct about feeling she wanted to dive deeper with her clients: according to her Soul Design, she had a need for creative solutions and depth, and her Expertise required a *highly intimate long-term journey* with her clients. But none of this could fit into an hour-long session!

So, we created a 6-month offer that gave room to all that Julie wanted to do with her clients. We priced that offer at $10k. We built that offer around the people she was meant to work with — the clients she already contracted with on the Soul level and now was positioned to attract on the material plane. This became a foundation of her methodology, so her message became streamlined. Her posts began to get traction on social media and people were inquiring about her work. She didn't feel any pressure or doubt in transitioning into selling a high-ticket offer because it felt so aligned to her Soul Design and natural. She signed her first $10k client just 4 weeks after.

Since then, she was able to let go of the one-off sessions completely. Many of her session-clients actually bought her higher priced offer — she just didn't have a unique program to offer them before and didn't know how to explain the value of her healing work, but once she did, many signed up. Julie grew past 6 figures with just 10 clients!

If you picked up this book because you're looking for this type of transformation, you'd be most interested in the parts of the Conscious F.U.T.U.R.E. Method in Part 2, Chapter 7, on Soul Design Strategy and messaging by Soul Expertise.

***

Or another common client story — let's call her Sofia.

She came to us feeling:
* stressed out from indecision;
* frantic in her creative energy;
* overcomplicating her business with multiple not-related offers.

Sofia would produce a new program three times per year at least because she lost interest in promoting it. She sold $1k offers over Instagram and DMs, it felt like magic would happen when she was inspired and excited about the new offer. Then, as her own energy fell, she couldn't close any sales — and so she'd move onto the next new offer. This kept her overwhelmed, inefficient, and confused about how to grow past her $100k level that she was barely able to stay at.

She had zero business strategy despite her success! She had no marketing strategy either. No methodology. No higher-end offer. No clarity on her unique expertise. She was amazingly creative, inspiring, sensual, and powerful — yet none of this resulted in anything sustainable.

Applying my methodology, it became clear that her Soul Design was of a creative person who needed to have room to be inspired, which her current business model did not provide. We uncovered her Soul Expertise of an Artist and Alchemist archetypes — she was awesome at activating creative and sensual energy naturally, by people just being in her space. This meant she was only able to sell when she was inspired and there was a different solution than the one she came up with. Hers was to just keep creating new offers and dumping the previous ones (highly wasteful!)

The new strategy we came up with was based on her Soul Expertise — we built her methodology and offer about creativity, sensuality and empowerment. This was a large enough category for her to be creative yet focused enough for being able to speak to a specific person. We priced that offer at $10k.

This was so naturally aligned with her Soul that Sofia didn't feel she was promoting an offer anymore — she was just being herself. This led to many inquiries, and with just 10 clients she was able to move past 6-figures. Sofia didn't have to create new offers anymore — this one offer was flexible enough to accommodate her creativity and get her paid well for doing her Soul Work in the world.

If you recognize yourself in this example, you'll want to read the part about Niche and market positioning later on in the book.

***

Or another common client story — let's call her Abby.

She came to us feeling so frustrated about her business — she was selling five different low-level offers for under $100, dabbling in three-four different niches (energy healing, sexuality, business), and trying to imagine how in the world she could get to her vision of being a Queen of a huge kingdom worth millions? As a new mom, she wanted to give priority to her child, but she was scared to stop selling her one-off sessions or low-end products. She was almost at $100k, but her current 'queendom' was held together by hard-work-hustle and pure audacity. She knew that there was no way she could get to where she full-heartedly knew she was meant to be from where she was. So, she joined my Conscious F.U.T.U.R.E. Mastery program.

Applying my methodology, we began to dig deep into what her superpower was — and we uncovered that it was about "talking with Fairies". Not surprisingly, this was not reflected in any of her current offers or products — she thought it might be "too woo" and no one would want to pay for it, especially for a higher-end price! Her Soul Design was of a Ruler archetype, a leader-powerhouse who could create what she envisioned, but she was right in the fact that she could not get into the millions by selling $100 things. The math just didn't make sense — especially for a young mom without a large list or a huge social media audience.

Here is what we did: we created an offer that was focused on the most lucrative niche for her (female small store owners) and included "fairies" as the main unique factor (yeap, she had to do some visibility clearing here!). We made sure the value of the offer was enormous and no-where-else available combination of grounded mentoring for what store owners needed with unique solutions they've never expected — she was positioning as the 'market of one'. We priced it at $12k. We got clear on the methodology behind it (she had it all along but never had clear words to describe it before!) We also created a smaller introductory offer for $1500 that led into the $12k offer, and consolidated all the smaller offers she previously had as bonuses and free gifts. She then hosted a free event to introduce people to her work and grow her list.

To her surprise, the biggest attraction to her work were these very 'Fairies' that she was hiding! People came out of the woodwork, joining the smaller program (including the ones who were already on her list and never purchased before) and a few signed up for the higher offer directly. Here is the change in her life: Abby now works only 3 days per week — and that includes coaching her clients, marketing by writing posts and creating livestreams on Facebook, and sales calls. The rest of her time was freed up for her baby, family life, and creative endeavors. And best of all, she got to do the thing she absolutely loved — talk to Fairies all day long and get paid for it!

Just six higher-end clients and a few more from the lower-end offer resulted in $100k income (while working about 70% less). It's clear that Abby, just like you could be, is positioned to quantum leap into her 'Queendom' with ease. All she had to do was refocus everything in her business around her unique Soul Expertise!

***

Let's look at one more example of transformation — let's call her Elizabeth.

Elizabeth came to us as most of our clients:
- ❖ Overworked and crazy busy with low-end clients;
- ❖ Underpricing herself;
- ❖ Confused about how to create her vision from where she was at now.

She was trying to sell what she knew how to do, weight loss, and it was falling flat. She felt she had to constantly convince her clients why they should lose weight, why her way was effective, why talking about this was not taboo… She felt a lot of pressure despite her successes! Elizabeth's five low-end product funnels and a few $3k offers managed to generate a $200k+ income — but at the price of being over-extended jumping around too many offers, stressed as she constantly had to deal with clients' not following her advice, ad spend that was eating at her profits, and scared she won't be able to keep it up much longer.

As soon as we started working together, we looked at her Soul Expertise — it was in helping women build a deep intimate relationship with themselves (mind, body, and Soul). Once we knew that, using my Conscious F.U.T.U.R.E. Methodology, it was obvious that her expertise had been incorrectly positioned in the marketplace. She was focusing on convincing women to lose weight instead of empowering the ones who already wanted to let go of extra baggage! We clarified her Soul Expertise and modified the target audience that would be way more receptive to what Elizabeth wanted to come through her.

We consolidated her jerry-rigged funnels into one overarching business strategy, where all her mini-courses and products led into one higher-end offer. We built that offer on her unique methodology of feminine empowerment and self-trust techniques (she already used it, but haven't had words for it).

When Elizabeth tried to scale her $200k+ business before, she just multiplied the hardship, ad spend, and stress. We helped Elizabeth to make her delivery process scalable — instead of a private program we created a rolling enrollment group offer that didn't have a set beginning and, thus, could accommodate an infinite number of incoming clients. We priced that offer at $7k. We rewrote her sales copy and her marketing for all her smaller products to lead into this one flagship offer. Before, her funnels were only selling smaller products and leading nowhere — now they were actually serving a purpose!

In just one month, applying the same social media strategies she used before she started with paid ads (like posting, free events, messenger, emails) Elizabeth was able to not only bring correct clients into her funnels (who desired the change without any convincing!) but also to lead them through her sequences into her higher end offer. This positioned her to scale into multi-6 figures while working only 2 hours per week! Once the automations were set up, it was simply a matter of showing up, presenting her message and having a public presence to promote her offer through free events that were pre-planned and easy to execute. We also helped her attract a rockstar team to free her to remain in her zone of genius.

What Your Life Could Be

You can start by realizing that you don't have to "work hard" to achieve success. You do have to be dedicated and committed, able to efficiently push and effectively hustle for a sprint when needed (such is entrepreneur's life!) but not for a marathon! In fact, the more aligned actions you perform, and the more in flow you are, the easier everything becomes. This includes attracting high-paying clients and creating abundance in all areas of your life.

1. One of the main factors in a harmonious Soul-led business is creating Wealth by your Soul Design (which naturally eliminates friction!)
2. The other is basing your marketing and message on your Soul Expertise (your innate God-given superpower)
3. And the third is consistent and efficient Action (your manifestation tool).

Here are some of the changes you can expect by implementing my Conscious F.U.T.U.R.E. Method.

❖ You feel such incredible confidence and alignment with marketing and selling your offer, able to fully be yourself without self-minimizing or apologizing for your unique badassery.
❖ You know exactly what to say in your social media content and emails that compels your ideal clients to come to you. No more random posting or over-teaching without results.

❖ Your energetics are at a whole new level of mastery. You don't get thrown around by your emotional waves anymore, able to stay in high frequency despite any circumstances, and elevate your manifestation capacity.

❖ Selling stops feeling like selling. You only speak with qualified prospects who want to work with you and can afford it, and you're able to quote your higher fees (without feeling like throwing up).

❖ You follow your own unique strategy that matches your Soul Design. You still do hard things when needed (it is personal transformation after all!) but you are building sustained momentum.

In the pages of this book, I will share with you the important factors and strategies at play when considering The Conscious F.U.T.U.R.E. Method. This book is your ultimate guide to unleashing the potential of your Soul-aligned strategy and creating consistent results that match the audacious Vision you have for your Mission.

I've poured my heart and Soul into outlining the important factors and strategies that you need to know — it's the asset you've been missing all along. But here's the thing — you can't just skim through this book and expect to get the full benefit. You need to read every single letter, from beginning to end.

Don't be the type who starts reading but never finishes or gets confused by skipping around. Let's dive in together and build on the terms and explanations so that you can radically change the nature of your business. It'll only take you an afternoon or three to finish, but the ideas and strategies that you'll unlock will be priceless and last a lifetime. Are you ready? Let's go!

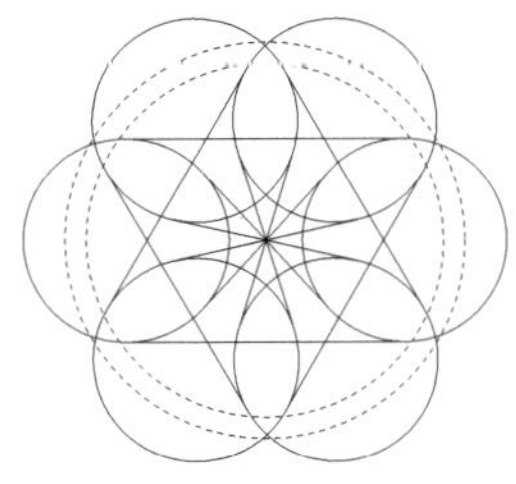

Chapter 2:

Recovering Overachiever: My Journey from Pressure to Sustainable Success

"I have not failed. I've just found 10,000 ways that won't work."

- THOMAS EDISON

Let me lay it all out for you, dear Soul sister. At the time I created this methodology, I was living a life that looked pretty damn good on paper. I had a thriving mentoring and healing business that kept me busy five days a week, with amazing clients that I truly loved helping. But deep down, I felt trapped and teetering on the edge of burnout, despite the fact that I was living my Soul Mission.

Every month, I was launching some new program, course, or event, and while they were all successful to various degrees, I felt depleted and drained. And to top it off, I had no clue how to market my services, so I was relying only on word-of-mouth to keep my business afloat.

Sure, I was making about $200k a year, but at what cost? I was working 12-hour days and charging $175 per 90 minutes of my life, booked a year in advance, and feeling zero joy in any of it. I was consumed by a toxic mix of anxiety, pressure, obligation, and pride. I was proud of how hard I could work, how much I could push myself, and how selfless I could be. And I was damn good at it, too! My clients were raving about me and I had over 700 die-hard fans promoting me to their circles. I had three best-selling books under my belt, was invited to speak at all sorts of conferences and podcasts, and led spiritual tours all over the world.

However, in reality I was frustrated, dissatisfied, and exhausted. Burnt out. Done. I had created this incredible Vision for my life, and on the surface, everything looked amazing. But the truth was, living this vision felt like trying to climb Mount Everest in flip flops. I was stuck, torn between not wanting to abandon my clients and knowing that I had to move on.

I took on ANY healing or mentoring client who needed me — how could I refuse? I am here to serve after all... If someone didn't feel super happy after their session, I could spend hours and hours agonizing over it, looking for proactive solutions, tuning into them, emailing them what I found out — yes, all for the price of a $175 session.

My life was predictable in the sense that once I got up, I was working with clients till I went to bed. I ate somewhere in between appointments — for 12 years it never occurred to me to schedule a lunch break!

I was addicted to the pressure — I call it "success by stoicism".

I am a very strong person (as I am sure you are too!) and the crazy thing is — I was actually living my Mission — serving clients and truly changing the world one person at the time.

Then why was I so freaking miserable??

Why did it have to be so HARD?

It took me hitting rock bottom not once, not twice, but THREE damn times to finally realize that something needed to change.

It wasn't until I started to really examine my business and my life *that I realized the problem was not with my clients or my Soul Work, but with the way I had structured my business.* I was operating from a place of sacrifice, putting clients' needs above everything and thus being grossly underpaid for the value I provided. I was also stuck in a mindset that told me I had to work hard and over-deliver in order to be successful.

I began to see that there was a different way of doing things, a way that would allow me to work with fewer Soul-aligned clients and charge higher prices, while diving way deeper and delivering even better results. I started to invest in myself and my business, learning about marketing and sales strategies that could help me reach more people and attract higher-paying clients. Not everything I've learned aligned with me, so I had to further modify, experiment, and invent my own version of a solution. Over the years, I've invested over $150k in my education to get clarity on my own methodology — so that I can help YOU.

It wasn't easy to make the shift, but it was worth it.

All my struggles were because I had unwittingly created a structure for my life and business that didn't align with my natural Soul Design. You see, it's not enough to just manifest an awesome business through hard work and pushing. You also need to choose the correct clients to work with so you are fulfilled and have no need to push! You need to know the right business and marketing strategies to keep it running smoothly. And if you're getting paid hourly, you're unknowingly capping your earning capacity. It might feel good to over-work and over-give because you're using your Soul gifts, but deep down, you know something's off. And the truth is, there is a better way.

And that's why I created this methodology — to help other spiritually ambitious, impatient women like me find a better way.

It all comes down to the structure and strategy of your business. Yeap, lots of work involved in growing a business to multi-6 figures and up — this is why there are so very few people who accomplished this! I'm not one of these coaches who tells her clients "just meditate, intend, and it will all happen for you". I think you and I both have been around the block enough times to know that business takes consistent work. But what kind of work — that is up to you.

I've got to tell you, I was always pretty damn successful in my life. Every business I started, and there's been 6 so far, always made a profit. And any client I chose to work with, well, they got results. But I would push so hard to make it work, to get those results for those clients.

And then it hit me… I was just so indiscriminate with my own gifts and who I chose to serve with them. I was saying 'yes' to anyone and everyone who came my way. And that was burning me out. That's when I realized that I needed to make some serious changes. And those changes became the backbone of what I now call my Conscious F.U.T.U.R.E. Method.

Right now, you might be someone who is trying to prove her worth through her success. You might think that if you get 20 more clients, or more social media followers, or another zero on your yearly income — then you will finally "make it". You might be subconsciously programmed to believe that by working harder and helping more people, you would be worthy of love, support, and abundance. But the reality is, you don't need to prove anything. You are already worthy, just as I was when I realized it!

I let go of the pressure.

I stopped trying to force success and started fully living from my Soul.

What does this mean? It means: speaking my truth, being choosy about who I serve, getting paid well for the extreme level of deep loving care and expertise I provide, and fully tapped into my inner knowing, intuition, superpowers, and natural flow.

And you know what? My business started to thrive even more. My clients were happier, I was happier, and I was making a bigger impact on the world.

And the funny thing is, I was actually teaching this method to my clients without even realizing it, and without fully following it myself! But once I did start to really embody these principles, everything changed for me. This was over a decade ago now.

Today, I have a thriving business that allows me to work with clients I love, charge prices that reflect the true value of my work, and have the time and energy to live a balanced and fulfilling life. I'm living my Soul Mission in a way that is truly aligned with my natural Soul Design.

If any of the struggles I've shared, the hustle mindset and operating from sacrifice as if its service sound familiar, then my message to you is this:

❖ Clear articulation of your unique expertise is crucial.
❖ Choosing the right clients is vital for your income AND happiness.
❖ Selling is NOT a bad thing and there is no need to sacrifice your Soul to market your business or generate revenue.
❖ Soul-aligned energetics paired with solid strategy create impact and wealth.
❖ Trust yourself, your gifts, and the Universe. You are worthy.
❖ There is no such thing as "not ready" on the Soul level. The best time to start upgrading what you've got (or just start!) was yesterday! The next best time is NOW.

When you live from that place of alignment, everything else will fall into place.

The 3 specific changes I've made that got my business to become a 7-figure Soul-led Empire:

1. Aligned everything to my Soul Design Strategy, chose the right clients, and simplified my business.
2. Started to market from my Soul Expertise instead of over-teaching from my knowledge and skills.
3. Shifted from low-end one-off-session hustle to high-ticket deep dives that my clients adore.

Self-Reflection for Achieving Success

Before we dive into the juicy stuff, let's check in and see where you're at in your business journey. Are you ready to rate yourself on a scale from 1 to 5, with 1 being "not accurate at all" and 5 being "most accurate"?

Don't worry, this isn't a test or anything like that — it's simply a way for us to get clear on where you're at so that we can create a plan that's tailored to your unique needs. Once you've rated yourself for each statement, we'll total up your scores and use the Answer Key to determine your next steps.

So take a deep breath, grab a pen, and let's get started!

SELF-REFLECTION STATEMENT	RATING
I am able to spend time with my family, and on my self-care, while my business makes money.	
I am 100% willing to do whatever it takes until it takes, I am committed.	
I have absolute certainty that I am capable of achieving my desired level of success in my business.	
My past experiences and failures have NO significant impact on my ability to succeed.	
I feel clear on HOW to reach my income Vision.	
I feel calm in my business and my marketing (opposite of chaotic, confused, overwhelmed, scared)	
I am NOT afraid of experimenting, testing, and taking risks in my business.	
I am focused and do NOT procrastinate when it comes to taking action on important tasks.	
I am visible online, my services are being sold daily through my content, via DMs, or through ads.	

I believe that I create the "perfect" moment and always take action regardless of feeling ready or not.	
For every 1 hour of information consumption, I spend 10 hours actively implementing.	
I am willing to challenge my own beliefs and assumptions, and to consistently step outside of my comfort zone in order to achieve my goals.	
I have one high-ticket offer that generates over 70% of my income.	
I do NOT have "shiny-object-syndrome" and don't jump around.	
My personal energetics and mindset are always in Abundance despite any external circumstances.	
TOTAL UP YOUR SCORE >>>	

What your score really means (the Answer Key):

SCORE: 1-20
Insecurity is Holding you Back

Dear Soul sister, you are at the place where your own beliefs, subconscious limitations, frantic rebellions, and fears are holding you back from brilliantly shining your Light and generating awesome income. And I'm so glad you're here because things are about to change!

Chances are, you are struggling with confusion, unable to find clarity in your magnificent Vision. You jump from one business strategy to the next or explore different niches without any clear direction. Or perhaps you are struggling to get your business off the ground, feeling like you don't know how to even start manifesting your Vision, lacking expertise and niche awareness.

Currently, you are missing business strategy, marketing strategy, niche and expertise clarity, and thus do not know how you are supposed to show up to manifest your business Vision. You are probably overwhelmed, stressed, and frustrated that what you desire feels so far away.

Look, I know how you feel. Many of my clients started right here, where you are right now.

More than anything, you have to decide to show up and own it!
- Stop minimizing yourself;
- Stop listening to inner critic and the not-enoughness fears;
- Stop apologizing for your great Vision;
- Stop letting the "not knowing HOW to do it" derail you. Get support!

The pages of this book will show you how you can replace all your negative beliefs with a proven system of integrous multi-D energetics and solid strategy that will solve 90% of your struggles. You'll want to pay extra attention to Part 2 and 3 when you get there.

What is required from you is commitment to seeing reality from a higher viewpoint — where your doubt is ALWAYS a liar and you, my dear, are a one-time-cosmic-event!

SCORE: 21-44
You're Trying too Hard

Well, my dear, it's likely that you've got yourself into a mindset of struggle in your business. You're hustling hard, trying all sorts of lead generation techniques and tactics, but still not quite nailing it when it comes to landing those high-ticket clients.

You might feel like you're doing everything "right" from a strategic point of view, but deep down, you're not sure how to boost your visibility, increase your sales, and charge those higher fees that you know you're worth.

Referrals might be your go-to method for landing clients, but you're not sure how to scale up and get more clients without working yourself into the ground. And let's not even get started on those multi-step funnels and messenger-selling templates that you've invested in — they just don't seem to be cutting it for you.

But here's the thing: it doesn't have to be this hard. The methodology I'm about to share with you can help you finally *break free from the struggle* and start landing those high-ticket clients with ease and integrity.

And even if you don't decide to work with me, remember this: your business strategies should always revolve around YOU. By simplifying your business, you can create the space and income you desire while making a massive impact.

So, let's do this — it's time to ditch the struggle and start living your best business life! Pay extra attention to Chapter 7 when you get there.

SCORE: 45⁺
Time to Scale Correctly

You, my dear, are on the right track to scaling your business and bringing your Vision to life. But as you continue to grow, you're finding yourself hitting some old beliefs that you thought you had already left behind, right? And let's face it, the business and marketing strategies that used to work for you might not be cutting it anymore.

You might still be struggling with sales, or feel like you still need to clarify your messaging, even though you're already getting great results. Or maybe you're clear on what you're doing but can't seem to scale it because you're afraid of leaving clients behind or not being able to provide the same level of service in a group setting as you do in 1:1.

At this level, it's not just about strategy (although it does need to be adjusted to match your next level). It's about refining your transformation, upgrading your clients, messaging, and offers, and elevating your frequency to match your actual Vision. It's time to get selective and fully respect your uniqueness. And don't forget to get support in the form of a team or automations, so you can focus on your zone of genius and scale successfully in a Soul-led way.

So let's do this, dear Leader! It's time to break through those old beliefs, implement correct business strategy, and bring your Vision to life in a way that truly aligns with your Soul.

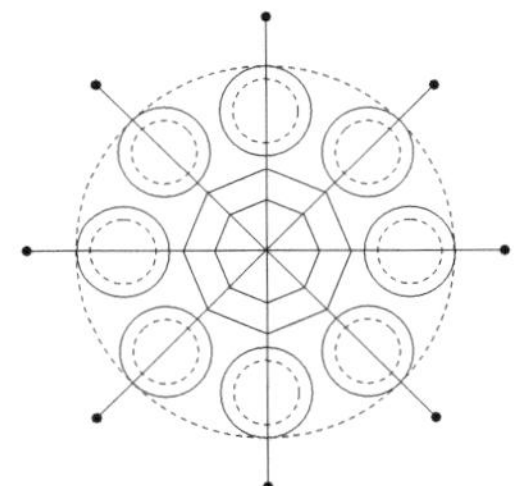

Chapter 3:

FOUR PROBLEMS AND HOW TO SOLVE THEM

"Step out of the history that is holding you back. Step into the new story you are willing to create."

- OPRAH WINFREY

88% of millionaires in the United States are self-made. You do not need to be born into wealth to become wealthy. The size of your success equates to how big you can dream and how committed you are to getting there. And it starts with looking into what might be holding you back from achieving your awesome badass Vision.

I'd like to walk you through the 4 most common challenges I see my clients face — and how they can be solved with my methodology — so you too can become the sought after and profitable leader you were born to be.

Why proven Business Strategies don't seem to work for *YOU* (despite supposedly working for 'everyone else').

My dear rebel Leader, it's time to look into why so many business strategies you try don't seem to work for you despite seemingly working fine for everyone else. Maybe you've invested in course after course, hoping that each one will finally show you the secret to creating the perfect funnel, or creating a client avatar, or writing posts that convert better. Or maybe you've signed up for a large program with lots of participants, thinking that if so many people bought it, it must be good. But then you start to study, and you feel defeated. It's all wrong, it's the same old thing you've seen before, just repackaged with better marketing.

And let's not forget those money-manifestation coaches who promise to heal your abundance karma or inability to receive for a hefty price of $10k or more. A few of them are awesome, and maybe it works for a while, and you do experience some inner transformation, but in the end, you're left with a nagging feeling that you are still not sure how to create the success you see others having, despite knowing that your work is incredible. And so you slide back to the old habits of pressure, over-work, and inner friction.

What *are* these 'proven' business strategies that "should" work for you?

- ❖ Live launching 4-6 times per year and feeling enormous pressure;
- ❖ Posting on social media ten times per day to convince your audience that they need your stuff, feeling exhausted;
- ❖ Dancing and pointing on Tik-Tok or showing your "back story" on Insta live all day long that just feels gross;

❖ Having to invent yet another freebie every week or a mini-course every month;
❖ Living on Messenger in fake conversations because supposedly this is how you should close the high-ticket sale if you want to avoid a normal video call;
❖ Creating huge free events to put thousands of new leads onto your list, only that no one buys your offer;
❖ 20 step funnels with lots of bumps and upsells that either kill your Soul or cost you as you have to outsource them without much ROI;
❖ Targeting paid ads to an automated webinar in hopes this will bring buyers, and either over-spending because 'you have to bear it out' despite lack of results, or freaking out and turning off the ads;
❖ Hard-close sales tactics to push the leads into buying because "this is the only way they will purchase".

This list makes your blood boil, right?

That's because true success and abundance aren't about a one-time cookie-cutter solution or quick fix. It's not only about integrity, it's about a fundamental shift in the way you approach your business and your life. This search for a "secret" that will finally open up the wealth flow for you — it's over.

YOU are the secret.

It's about adopting an entirely new way of being, one that's aligned with your true purpose and values, with your Soul Design.

Later in this book, I'll show you how amazing this can be!
For now, take a moment to check in with yourself.

Self-Reflection for Business Strategy:

We're not here to test you, so don't worry. This is just another tool to help us understand your current situation better. All you have to do is rate yourself on a scale of 1 to 5 for each statement, with 1 being "not accurate at all" and 5 being "most accurate".

Once you're done, we'll tally up your scores and use the Answer Key to guide you towards your next steps. So take a moment to relax, grab a pen, and let's begin!

SELF-REFLECTION STATEMENT	RATING
I do NOT jump on every fast-track tactic that shows up in my feed.	
I never follow someone else's strategy without customizing it to my unique needs first.	
I listen to my intuition as much as I listen to my mind when it comes to business strategy.	
I never reject a suggested strategy based on discomfort or fear, only if it is NOT in integrity or does not light me up.	
I am able to generate $10k-$50k per month in the way that fits me and is fully aligned to me, without pressure.	
I know exactly what to do to grow my income in a way that feels right (without forcing myself into cookie-cutter strategies I saw others do).	
I feel confident in my ability to implement a new business strategy even if I have to learn, test, and step outside of my comfort zone.	
My philosophy is about looking inside for answers, and finding a correct coach/mentor to help implement what we both see fits me (instead of chasing trending tactics).	

If I wanted to, I know exactly how I could generate $20k-$100k revenue without live-launching multiple times per year.	
My social media content is a part of a larger business strategy and is managed daily by me, automations, or a VA (instead of random-posting without strategy).	
I never feel that I have to do something that is *not aligned* to get the results.	
I know the difference between "not aligned" and my own fear of visibility or experimenting.	
I do NOT follow the opinion or advice of someone who is not at least 10 steps ahead of me.	
I am crystal clear on my expertise and what I offer.	
I have a clear path that a prospect follows from the moment they enter my world (social media > free gift > community/email list> low-end product > high-end product) — all my offers are linked.	

TOTAL UP YOUR SCORE >>>

What your score really means (the Answer Key):

SCORE: 1-20
Fundamentals are Missing

Well, my dear, let me just cut straight to the chase here: your business is missing some major foundational pieces that are essential for long-term success. And I know you feel it — the exhaustion, fear, frustration, confusion, and lack of confidence that comes with trying to make things work without all the pieces in place.

But listen up, Soul sister, it's not your fault. You've probably been trying to implement someone else's ideas and strategies that just don't align with your Soul Design or Vision. And let me tell you, that's a recipe for disaster.

But don't you worry, because I've got some good news for you! You have the power to redesign and establish these fundamentals from the ground up. And trust me, dear fellow rebel, it's going to be worth it.

What you'll learn in Part 2 of this book can take your business to the multi-6-figure level and bring you the success you've been dreaming of. All it takes is an **open mind and a willingness to make some changes**. So go ahead, read on, and get ready to experience a huge transformation in your business. *You've got this!*

SCORE: 21-44
Adjustments are Needed

Hey precious, if your score landed you here, it means an *incoherent business strategy* and a *confusing marketing message* are holding you back from rapid growth and peace in your business. Something's not quite clicking in your business strategy and marketing approach. I get it — it's frustrating to rely on un-sustainable marketing methods and feel like you're talking to the wrong people or saying all the wrong things. But let me tell you, there's a better way!

With this book, you can find the perfect hook for your marketing and attract the right audience who truly understands and values what you do. No more low-ticket sessions and vampire clients — you'll be able to replace them with higher-ticket offers and dream clients who are perfectly matched to your expertise. And the best part? You'll actually enjoy what you do again, because you'll be working in a way that feels totally aligned with YOU.

You'll be able to market and deliver your offers without pressure or forcing yourself into strategies that don't fit you.

So, get ready to uplevel your business. Say goodbye to feeling like you just "own a job" and hello to owning a business that's fully aligned with your values and expertise. You'll have more time for self-care and you'll be able to increase your revenue like never before. It's time to take back control and live the life you've always dreamed of.

SCORE: 45⁺
Time to Uplevel

It looks like you've got your main signature offers dialed in and you're feeling pretty good about your business strategy. But you know there's more out there for you — you're ready to elevate your frequency, uplevel your strategy, and scale this thing as quickly as possible. And let me tell you, dear badass rebel Leader, this book is here to help.

The biggest hurdle for you right now is figuring out the next level strategy and energetics. You've hit a ceiling with your current strategy, and you know it's time to make some changes. But where do you start?

That's where Part 2 comes in, my dear. We'll help you get even more aligned with who you truly are and what you're meant to do in this world, while adjusting your business strategy to be the most sustainable and Soul-led possible. In Part 3, you'll find the correct energetics and mindset needed to get you there.

With our guidance, you'll be able to readjust your strategy to fit your unique needs and find a clear path to multiply your already amazing results. You'll have an awesome team to support you and the fuel you need to set your business on fire. So don't wait — read on (don't skip ahead, remember, each chapter builds on the previous one) and get ready to take your business and message to the next level!

Why, despite your best explanations about what you do (and being really good at doing it), no one outside of your circle really gets what you're saying.

Listen up, lady. I know you're out there, crushing it and making a difference in this world. You're not just talented — you're freaking phenomenal. You hold the power to elevate the collective consciousness and change the game for humanity. You've got unique codes within you that this world is waiting for, and it's time to step up and answer the call.

You're not just here to play small, or hide behind your fears, or work yourself to the bone. You're here to do the transformative work that the world desperately needs — whether that's as a Healer, Mentor, Coach, or Conscious Leader. You were born for this, Soul sister. You've got gifts that the world is starving for, and it's time to unleash them in full force.

And let's be real, you already know how amazing you are. You feel it in your bones, and it's written all over your face. So don't hold back, don't dim your light, and don't let anyone else tell you what you're capable of. You know who you are and what you're here to do, and it's time to unleash that magic and change the world.

The problem is… no one really gets what you're saying.

Oh, my dear, I feel you. Trying to explain your brilliance and value to potential clients can be frustrating as hell. You pour your heart and Soul into every detail of what you do, how you do it, and why it is so important, but somehow it still falls flat. And then you start over-explaining, trying to pack in every little specific term and detail that makes sense to you, but only ends up confusing your prospects even more. It's a vicious cycle that can leave you feeling defeated and questioning your worth.

But let me tell you something — it's not your fault. The problem isn't that what you do isn't clear or valuable — it's that you haven't yet found the words to truly connect with your ideal clients. You haven't yet tapped into the language, messaging, and methodology that will truly resonate with them and make them feel seen and understood.

Here are some examples of what this sounds like:

"I help clients experience harmony and live their best life."

"I activate your intuition and help you find balance and prosperity."

"I do chakra balancing."

"I help you lose weight and feel your best."

"I help women feel better and have energy for an amazing life."

"I do breathwork to release limitations that hold you back."

"I help women have better health that is aligned to their Soul Light."

"I support women in personal transformation and relationships."

"I help people understand their astrology cycles."

"I guide people to have great relationships, health, and abundance."

> *"I do EFT to relieve anxiety, lose weight, manifest abundance, and feel confident."*

> *"I empower business owners to be free of scarcity mindset and open."*

NONE of these will sell at the premium level.

Sorry if I am saying something you might have been saying... but you can see how unclear this is, right? This is the reason that it feels so hard to sell anything!

Or maybe you are saying this:

> *"I work with archangel Rafael, I help people clear their chakras on the crystalline level and adjust their karmic path through the 3rd dimension with energy healing, channeling, EFT, and breathwork."*

> *"I do intermittent fasting to help you to improve your overall health, lose weight, have more vitality, feel good about yourself, and unlock your full potential."*

> *"I am an ordained priestess of the Divine Order of Golden Light from the 5th dimension, and I am here to help you manifest your best life by integrating golden-string codes of abundance from Pleiades."*

> *"I hold space for couples to connect and use EFT, the Gottam Method, and evidence-based techniques to increase your joy and feeling like you are one."*

> *"I work with the angels and loving spirits to help you love yourself, activate your 10D love resonance, expand the range of your ability to love other people, and step into your role as a cosmic guide of Love on Earth."*

This is what over-explaining looks like (that no one understands!)

NONE of these will sell at the premium level either.

People don't care about what you do.

> Yeap, they just don't. They care about how you can help them achieve their desired outcome or transformation. Aka "what is in it for THEM?!"

Few in this coaching space want to talk about this *messaging problem* because even fewer have a real solution for overcoming it. In this book, I'll not only show you **how to overcome the 'confused audience' problem, but I'll show you how to set yourself apart as the true 'market of one'** — positioning based on your unique methodology.

We'll talk more on that later, but for now, it's worth taking a moment to ask yourself the hard questions.

Self-Reflection for Methodology and Premium Offer:

Hey there! Let's get started with some self-reflection, shall we? Don't worry, I'm not here to judge you. Instead, I want to offer you a helpful tool to better understand YOUR current situation.

All you need to do is rate yourself on a scale of 1 to 5 for each statement. It's easy-peasy! Just choose 1 if the statement is "not accurate at all", and 5 if it's "the most accurate", with everything else in between.

Once you're done, we'll add up your scores and use the Answer Key to guide you towards your next steps. So, take a deep breath, grab a pen, and let's get on with it.

SELF-REFLECTION STATEMENT	RATING
At the end of the sales call or email/DM conversation, my potential clients are super clear on the value of my offer, and why they should purchase it.	
I am able to clearly explain my work in a way that connects with the needs and desires of my ideal clients.	
I have one main signature offer that clearly reflects my methodology, sourced by my expertise and Soul Mission.	
My methodology is reflected in my marketing and the signature offer, it defines a clear process and simplifies my work when I explain it to my potential clients.	
I strive to make it easy for potential clients to understand what I offer (instead of over-teaching about what I do).	
I prioritize speaking to the heart and Soul of my ideal clients, balancing their needs/desires with their logical mind requirements.	
I am comfortable experimenting, adjusting my target audience/my message, or my offer if it is not resonating with potential clients.	
I have a clear understanding of the desired practical and tangible outcome that my potential clients are seeking.	
I feel confident that if I asked my clients what I do, they will be able to describe it (all saying about the same thing).	

I am able to summarize what I do in such a way, that a 7-year-old could understand.	
I never over-explain. I only explain my work to the level that is necessary or asked for by my prospect.	
I know exactly what the difference is between "marketing message" and what I actually do for my clients once they sign up.	
I am able to focus on ONE thing my prospect needs to hear in order to choose to sign up for my offer, without feeling the need for a complete explanation.	
I do NOT customize for every client in every way, I have a system and I only customize within it.	
I fully embody the wealth energetics of higher fees, feeling confident to charge well for my unique methodology.	

TOTAL UP YOUR SCORE >>>

What your score really means (the Answer Key):

SCORE: 1-20

Not sure what to Do or Say

Well, let's get real for a moment. Right now, you're in a space where there's NO clear definition of who you are or what you offer. You're just going with the flow, selling whatever naturally sells without any real strategy behind it.

You're probably trying to attract more clients, improve your income, and feeling a bit frazzled and overwhelmed (or maybe even underworked and freaking out about why things aren't working despite your best efforts!)

I know, it's a tough place to be. You're constantly wavering between feeling like a total badass with a massive Mission to accomplish, and feeling like a nobody, thinking that everything has already been done before and that you'll never stand out from the crowd.

But let me tell you, dear fellow rebel Leader, you're at a crossroads. You can either tell the world to back off and claim your unique God-given awesomeness, or you can conform and blend in with the rest of the crowd, changing your message with every trend in the hopes of taking your business to the next level.

It's time for a "come to Jesus moment" (or Goddess/ Buddha/ Allah/ Brahma/ Yahweh/ Sacred Spirit, whatever), and really OWN who you freaking are! You're amazing, and you need to organize that awesomeness into a solid methodology. Because without it, my dear, you won't be able to sell your offers at the higher-ticket prices you're dreaming of.

In this book, I'll show you exactly what you need to do to finally get clear on your process, and position yourself to actually market and sell your offers with confidence (instead of feeling like you have multiple personalities, trying to juggle all your different skills and offerings!)

SCORE: 21-44
Trying to do it all

Are you finding yourself marketing to a wide audience, but still not quite sure who your ideal client is? I get it, sometimes we don't want to limit ourselves, but the truth is that being too broad can actually hinder your success.

You may be wearing many hats and using a plethora of techniques and modalities, but do your potential clients really need to know all of that? The reality is that you may be trying to prove yourself and back up your expertise with all these certifications and studies, but it's only you who needs convincing. Your clients will follow your lead, so if you believe you need to prove yourself, they will challenge you to do so.

But don't worry, I've got your back, Soul sister! In this book, I'll show you exactly how to focus your energy, beliefs, message, and words so that your prospects clearly understand what you're selling and are dying to work with you. Let's ditch the vicious cycle and step into our power, shall we?

SCORE: 44+
Strategize your Message

So it sounds like you've got some clarity on who you're selling to and what you're selling — that's amazing! But maybe you're feeling like your messaging is a bit all over the place. Sometimes it works, sometimes it doesn't, and you're not quite sure what the key to success is.

I bet you're more of an intuitive when it comes to messaging — inspired rather than strategic. And that's totally fine! But it's time to put some structure around it so that you have messaging that can be replicated, reused, and nothing goes to waste. Right now, you're probably saying everything and hoping something sticks. But with some systems and structures in place, you'll be able to take your business to the next level and skyrocket your success.

In Part 2, I'll show you exactly what you need to clean up to finally get there with ease, flow, and momentum building. You'll be feeling so good, so natural, and so Soul-aligned — *you've got this!*

Do you Dread the Sales Calls?
(And What This Means)

Let's talk about sales, shall we? I mean, you're either totally obsessed with it, or you dread it like a root canal. Maybe you even hate it so much you'd rather stick a fork in your eye than promote your own business!

But here's the thing — if you're not all in on sales, you're seriously holding yourself back from hitting that multi-6-figure mark and beyond. So, what's it gonna be? Time to step up and own your sales game like the badass magical Leader you are!

How many times have I heard from my clients when we're just starting to work together:

"I am sick of people constantly posting "buy my stuff" on social media! I put a sales link on my post very rarely so I don't look salesy."

"I try to avoid selling my program directly, saying stuff like "I want to hear from you" or "leave a comment".

"I hate sales calls — it just feels so hard, like I am asking for money".

"I don't know what to say on the call when they tell me they need to go think about it. I let them go, but they never return."

"I was told that follow up is everything and given a template to follow, but it feels like I am just chasing people! I hate this!"

"I get a lot of 'I don't have the money' and it is so frustrating!"

"It hurts to keep being rejected, over and over… so I try to avoid sales calls."

"I tried to outsource the sales calls, but the agency had a horrible close rate for my offer".

Okay, let's get real here. Sales can feel like an absolute nightmare if you're doing it wrong. I mean, who wants to feel like they're manipulating their potential clients, cornering them, or pressuring them into something they don't want to do? It's no wonder so many spiritual coaches, mentors, and healers struggle with sales!

And that's where things start to fall apart.

Because when you're afraid to sell, you're essentially holding yourself back from attracting the clients you need to grow your business and increase your income.

And let's be real, dear conscious Leader — that's not what you're here for. You're here to make an impact, help others, and create a life of abundance and fulfillment for yourself.

So, how can you start to break free from these limiting beliefs and step into your power as a sales queen? Don't worry, we'll get there in Part 2. But first, let's dig a little deeper into what's holding you back.

Okay, let's break it down. Here are some of the negative masculine subconscious patterns that might be holding you back and causing you to associate sales with all kinds of icky feelings:

1. Believing that you have to be pushy or aggressive to make sales, like you have to scream from the rooftops and force people to buy your stuff.

2. Thinking that you have to chase after potential clients, instead of attracting them naturally through your message and your brand.
3. Feeling like you have to cold-message or cold-call people who don't know you, which can be really uncomfortable and can feel like an invasion of their privacy.
4. Believing that you have to guilt people into realizing that you're the solution to their problem, which can be really manipulative and can erode trust.
5. Feeling like you have to manipulate people into parting with their hard-earned money, instead of providing real value and helping them to see the benefits of investing in themselves.
6. Believing that you have to put down other coaches or position yourself as 'better than them', in order to make sales.

Or the top 3 most typical rebellious, negative feminine "solutions" to the patriarchal programming patterns:
1. Believing that you don't need to sell at all, and that clients will just magically find their way to you without any effort or promotion on your part. This is a classic case of wishful thinking, and it's unlikely to lead to sustainable success in your business.
2. Allowing potential clients to walk all over you and dictate the terms of the sales process (like telling you *"I have to tune in, commune with my guides, think about it"*), even if it means you're losing out on opportunities to serve them and grow your income.
3. Feeling guilty or ashamed about charging for your services, and allowing clients to guilt-trip you into giving away your work for free or at a discount.

I'm here to put your worries to rest. Marketing and selling does not have to feel like that at all. The way I teach my clients to do this is SO natural that it doesn't even feel like they are marketing or selling.

Self-Reflection for Sales

So, let's check where you are on this… Remember, the same process — 1 through 5.

SELF-REFLECTION STATEMENT	RATING
I never chase clients, I believe in delivering value first and attracting ideal clients through my content.	
I go through a self-assessment after every sales call, and I measure only what I am in control of.	
I never try to control, manipulate, or push the potential client on the sales call.	
I have a clear strategy and show up "in charge" from the very beginning of every sales call.	
I know specific objections my prospects might have even before we get on the sales call, and know how to position myself as "different" than what didn't work for them before.	
On the sales call, I am easily able to show a potential client (without feeling bad, judging, or guilting) where she is off in her self-assessment or doesn't see her problem.	
I do NOT see objections as a problem, I am always ready to offer clarifications and support.	
I am known in the marketplace as a highly knowledgeable, trustworthy, and in integrity coach/healer.	
I have a specific strategy to support potential clients on the sales calls without over-giving.	
My sales calls are between 15-60 minutes, I typically don't run past that time, unless they are in the process of paying.	

My prices are in the top 10% of my industry, and I easily get paid what I ask for.	
I NEVER hear an objection "this is too much money".	
I close at least 30% of my sales calls from complete strangers (every third call).	
I actively create sales assets that overcome objections before I ever have one-to-one conversations when selling.	
I regularly show up on social media with a clear call-to-action, leading to buying from me. I never avoid mentioning that I have something they can sign up for!	
TOTAL UP YOUR SCORE >>>	

What your score really means (the Answer Key):

SCORE: 1-20
Sales Beginner

Hey there. If you're here reading this, chances are that sales is not your forte just YET. But hey, that's okay! So many people start here, held back by all sorts of limiting beliefs, fears, and even karmic baggage from past lives...

The good news is that if you're reading this book, you're ready to take your business to the next level, and beyond the six-figures into the realm of real Wealth and influence that you deserve. But that can only happen if you're willing to face your sales issues head on.

The truth is, you're struggling with sales because you've got beliefs that are holding you back and limiting your success. On top of that, you're likely confused about what sales really is, which can lead you to avoid it like the plague or to try to force your prospects into buying, which only leaves you feeling out of integrity and icky. And, my dear Soul sister, I totally get it — that's not the way to do things.

But fear not, in this book I'm going to show you exactly what needs to change in how you approach sales so that it's no longer a stumbling block for you. It's time to step into your power and unleash your potential. So go ahead, keep reading, and get ready to take your business to new heights!

SCORE: 21-44
Sales Hustler

If you're reading this, it's likely because you're selling your butt off, but somehow it's just not working the way you want it to. You've tried all the sales techniques, from specific CTAs to sales scripts, but you're still not seeing the results you deserve, or you are, but they don't feel right.

What if I told you that the problem is more complex than you think? What if I said that what's masquerading as a sales problem might actually be a messaging problem? And what if those "abundance blocks" or "money blockages" are really just a combination of an unclear methodology, confusing message, and lack of proper sales structure?

But you're here, Leader, because you're ready to get all of this sorted once and for all, and finally rock your sales like the boss Queen you are. This means not only mastering the art of sales calls, but also attracting pre-sold prospects to those calls by implementing steps to filter out those who aren't a good fit. You're right at the cusp of a breakthrough, my dear!

And that's where I come in. In this book, I'm going to give you the structure you need to make it all happen. The methodology I'm about to share will serve as your trusty guide to the correct flow, and I can't wait to support you every step of the way. So, let's make those sales!

SCORE: 44⁺
Sales Queen ready for the Next Level

If you're landed here, you know how to sell. You might not love it, but you know it. Or you might even find it easy enough. You already know how to speak to your ideal client, what to say to help convert them, how to handle objections — you've heard it all and you know what to do with it.

Or at least you've done it before, and I didn't kill you. You had faced fears, insecurities and doubt, and you've come out victorious. Congratulations on that!

Now is the time to take this to the next level. Your issue might not be in the sales process itself, but rather in over-customizing or lacking clarity in other areas like your high-ticket offer and delivery, your methodology, or your team support.

Don't worry, though — I've got your back. We'll dive deeper into these components in the book and help you take your sales game to new heights. Are you ready? Let's go!

Where to Find High Ticket Clients?

I can't tell you how many times I've had this conversation with women who are interested in joining my Conscious F.U.T.U.R.E. Mastery program. They're always saying things like:

> *"My audience can't afford a $5k program, where am I going to find people who can?"*

"My current clients complain about a $500 session, where will I find people to buy my $8k program?"

"I know my program is worth $10k, but I don't want to only work with rich people."

"I'm selling a $12k offer, but I want more clients at this level, where are they hiding?"

No matter if you are already selling $10k+ offers or if you are just thinking of creating your first one, you might be having the same question as everyone else is asking: WHERE are these high-ticket clients and HOW can I find them?

But here's the thing, my dear conscious Leader. There are some big misconceptions about high-ticket offers and sales that are holding you back:

❖ You think "high-ticket" means "expensive".
❖ You assume only rich people buy high-ticket programs.
❖ You believe you have to search for these potential clients in some special place.

Let me set the record straight. My clients understand that "high-ticket" doesn't mean "expensive" — it means "premium". Expensive is just a matter of perception, and in Wealth Energetics, there's no such thing as scarcity or comparison. Everything is one and forever abundant. So, there's no such thing as "expensive", just what is aligned or not aligned.

Unfortunately, many coaches have been teaching their clients to raise their prices as high as possible, even if it's not in integrity, just to appear more 'advanced'. But in reality, most of those offers were just overpriced. Adding a zero to a $500 offer and marketing it as a $5000 offer doesn't make it a high-ticket offer — just an overpriced one!

Now, let's talk about who buys high-ticket offers.

It's not just rich people. Most of my clients weren't rich when they started working with me, but they, probably just like you who's reading this book, were premium people. What does that mean? Premium clients are aligned with a high-ticket offer. They're self-responsible action-takers who have already studied the subject in various low-end ways and achieved results. They're looking for customized support and a shortcut to the next level, and they can afford the time, energy, dedication, and investment it takes to make it happen.

So, where do you find these premium level clients?

The best kept secret is that they're ALREADY in your audience, online in your communities, and in your personal circle. You just need to learn how to speak to them in a way that THEY want to work with YOU.

That's where Part 2 comes in. I'll show you how to change your language and call out to these premium level clients who are happy to pay your high-ticket prices and achieve great results. This way, instead of chasing clients, convincing people to see the value in your work, or pressuring them to buy, they will be coming to you, already pre-sold, ready to make a decision.

I'll give you more specific tools and examples in the coming chapters, but for now, take a moment to reflect on this topic.

Self-Reflection for High-Ticket Clients

SELF-REFLECTION STATEMENT	RATING
I am comfortable charging high-ticket prices ($10k+) that reflect the value of my offer.	
I don't market to everyone, I am clear about what kind of client is ideal for my specific offer, and I have a system to filter out people who do not match.	
I only speak to my ideal client, using specific words that they need to hear.	
I know in what specific way high-ticket messaging is different from low-ticket messaging.	
I am confident in my ability to attract premium clients who are willing and able to invest in themselves.	
I know how to position my high-ticket offer in the marketplace to attract premium clients.	
I am highly familiar with my ideal premium client psychographics, aspirations, and unique needs, and actively use this information in my messaging.	
I am skilled at communicating the value of my high-ticket offer in a way that resonates with premium clients.	
I know how to build trust and establish credibility with potential premium clients.	
I am confident in my ability to sign clients at a high-ticket level.	
I can clearly define the tangible outcome of my offer and connect it to my dream client's needs.	
I am able to articulate what makes me unique in a way that my potential premium clients can understand and are compelled to respond to.	

I know what type of person will have amazing results in my program.	
I am highly selective in who I invite into my high-ticket program.	
I know exactly what to say to attract my dream clients.	

TOTAL UP YOUR SCORE >>>

What your score really means (the Answer Key):

SCORE: 1-20
Need a High-Ticket Message

My dearest friend, it's time for you to uplevel — not just your message, but also yourself. You're at a point where you don't know how to attract those high-ticket clients, and you don't have anything for them to buy into either. But you want to, oh so badly!

You know deep down that you're meant to play at the top level, but you're still struggling to figure it all out. You're confused, scared, unsure of your message or expertise, and you just want to be who you're meant to be. Believe me, many of my clients have been there too.

But here's the thing — the dream in your heart is real, and it's absolutely possible for you to achieve it. However, it's going to take some work on your part — personal transformation that will elevate your frequency and uplevel your message and marketing strategy. But if you're up for the challenge, then I'm here to guide you every step of the way.

In this book, I'll show you exactly what you need to do to break into the premium market and attract those high-ticket clients with ease. Are you ready to take the plunge and transform into the powerhouse you're meant to be? Let's do this!

SCORE: 21-44
Must Fine-tune your High-Ticket Message

You're in a place where you know you're undercharging for your high-ticket offer, and deep down, you know it's worth so much more than what you're currently asking for. You're a rockstar and you deserve to be compensated accordingly! But you're also feeling a bit unsure about what raising your prices could mean for your business. It's natural to feel hesitant about rocking the boat, but if it doesn't feel right, it's time to make a change.

You recognize that you need to start speaking differently to attract a higher caliber of client. You've had some not-so-great clients in the past, and you know that not everyone gets amazing results with your current pricing. You have a vision for the kind of clients you want to work with, but you're not sure how to make that your main source of income or if it's even possible.

I totally get it, and I'm here to help you navigate this next level of your business. In this book, I'm going to guide you through the process of raising your prices and attracting the clients you love working with. We'll dive deep into what it means to create a congruent business that aligns with your values and helps you grow in a way that feels right for you. So let's get started on this exciting journey together!

SCORE: 44+
Time to Pour the Fuel on this Fire

If you're reading this, chances are you've got your strategy and selling game down pat. You've got your high ticket offer in place and you know how to communicate its value to your ideal clients. But for some reason, something just isn't clicking. Perhaps you're not getting as many clients as you'd like and you're starting to doubt whether your message, pricing, or strategy is really hitting the mark. Or maybe you're attracting the right leads, but you're having trouble turning them into paying clients.

I've seen this happen so many times before. Sometimes, we unknowingly sabotage our own success because deep down, we don't feel confident in the offer we're putting out there. It's time to take a step back and fine-tune your offer and methodology so you can attract and sign on the clients you really want.

In this book, we'll dive deeper into how to do just that. Let me take you away from all these problems to the secret key that will unlock your success! Excited? Let's go.

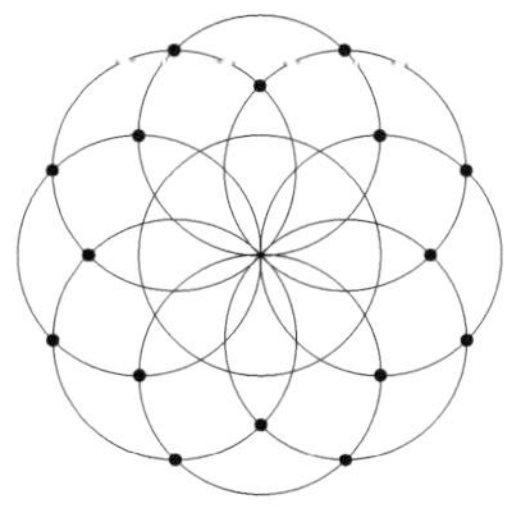

Chapter 4:

THE ONE DOMINO TO TOPPLE THEM ALL

"Wealth and Knowledge are like the two wings of a bird. Without either one, you will never fly."

- PTAHHOTEP, VIZIER OF EGYPT, 5TH DYNASTY,
"THE MAXIMS OF PTAHHOTEP" 2494 BC

Are you feeling like a hot mess with all the moving parts in your business? I totally get it! Sometimes it can feel like there's a million and one things to take care of before you can hit that next level of success.

But fear not my dear, because I am here to swoop in and simplify it all for you! Let's strip away the complexity and overwhelm and get you on track to the epic success you deserve.

Ready?

To sustainably grow to multi-6 or 7-figures, without pressure or forcing yourself into rigid cookie-cutter strategies, these five components must be in place in your Soul-led business:

❖ Clarity on your natural Expertise/superpowers and who you have Soul contracts with.
❖ Unique methodology that positions you as a "market of one" and articulates the value of your Soul Work.
❖ Compelling high-ticket offer with a streamlined delivery that lights you up.
❖ Perfect words your ideal client needs to hear to want to buy from you.
❖ Emotional, Mindset and Energetic Mastery to become highly visible in an elevated frequency range.

I can hear you thinking, *"But Eugenia, I've been trying to figure this out forever! I've explored my abilities, integrated them into my services as much as I could, I tried different niches, and even raised my fees, but the struggle and pressure never seem to end! How do I arrive at something that feels like I've made it and can finally relax?"*

Well, my friend, I have one thing for you that will topple ALL four of these struggles: my *Soul Design Strategy*, and specifically, its component called the **Future Identity**. *This is where you DECIDE who you want to be and how you want your business to unfold from the start.* Yeap — AHEAD of time!

In this book, I'll reveal my secret methodology for incorporating this Future Identity energetics of your Soul Design into every aspect of your life and business strategy. This will not only give you room to breathe but also Quantum-leap you into the multi-6 and even 7 figures with ease.

So buckle up, get ready to fly high, and let's unleash your true potential like never before — this time, WITHOUT the struggles.

Cure your Niche Struggles and Only work with Who you're Born to Serve

As I mentioned earlier, a component of your Soul Design — *Future Identity* — is the key to creating flow in your business, so you can manifest the next step of your huge Vision with EASE. **Deciding who you are going to show up as from now on** makes attracting ideal clients effortless. It resolves any Niche struggles once and for all, and allows you to resonate at the correct frequency that matches your Soul Mission.

Dear Leader, let me tell you something: all of this advice to choose your niche based on external factors is just a distraction. Mental analyzing, relying on statistics, copying others — it all makes you think that the answer is outside of you.

And so, you fall victim to Shiny Object Syndrome, jumping from one fascination to the next, buying every $47 course and checking up every marketing guru who promises to help you find the most lucrative niche. You over-teach on free events to prove your expertise, then overcompensate on delivery to prove your worth.

But all of this just leads to confusion and constant switching of niches, as your subconscious mind searches for what you're supposed to do and who you're supposed to work with to finally feel like enough.

You might be clear on your superpowers but still not sure how to fully monetize them, wondering if people will actually pay high-ticket for it. Or maybe you know exactly what makes you awesome, but are still struggling to make it the centerpiece of your business. You got to where you are today by working hard and learning certain skills, but deep down, you know that those things don't really light you up. Or this Niche thing might be a thorn in your side. You feel like you can help everyone, and the idea of narrowing down your audience feels limiting. But let's be real, you secretly know that this rebellion is holding you back from delivering your awesome gifts and getting paid higher fees with ease.

The truth is — the answer lies within.

And this is why, my dear magical badass Leader, **deciding on who you are going to show up as AHEAD OF TIME** is so important — it determines the quality of experience you are going to have with your Niche, and everything else in your business.

I will tell you more about how to construct this Future Identity, and how you can start on this right away, in Chapter 8, but don't skip Chapter 7 where I will show you more details overall about your Soul Design Strategy.

Uplevel Beyond Competition and Become the 'Market of One'

Let's be real here, dear rebel Leader, if you're not intentionally deciding who you're going to show up as, you're setting yourself up for a world of comparisonitis, self-doubt, and a never-ending to-do list. It's a recipe for misery and burnout.

Let me share something powerful with you. Through my methodology, you will step into your Future Identity and realize that you are already the person you were meant to be according to your Soul Design. This means that the ideal clients who are waiting for you are also waiting for the real, authentic, and aligned version of yourself.

By embodying your Future Identity, you will naturally attract these people and serve them at the highest level.

When you make a conscious decision about who you're going to be (and don't worry, I've got you covered on how to start this process in Chapter 9), you leave all that crap behind. No more trying to prove yourself, no more over-explaining, no more pressure to be something you're not. Instead, you step into your authority and become a magnet for your ideal clients.

If you're anything like me, you know that putting other people down to make yourself look good is not your style. Winning over someone else doesn't give you joy. However, this doesn't mean you don't like winning. You compete with yourself, always striving to outdo your previous achievements by keeping yourself to the highest standards.

It's easy to get sucked into this comparison game though, but let me tell you, it's a losing game. Depending on your personality, you might push harder, put enormous pressure on yourself to re-do everything you have, hire freelancers to do all the design and production, and just shove your fears down, override them, and step on yourself to launch your program anyway. And what happens? You record a perfectly polished 20-module course, pour your heart into it, spend months refining it to make it look and work just right, and yet when you finally put it out there... crickets. Not a single person buys it.

Or, you might find your excitement deflating. You start to believe that you're just like everyone else, that there's nothing special about you or your program. You convince yourself that no one will want this new thing, and that you should have just stuck with what was working already. You keep selling the old offer that doesn't really light you up, and you start to feel defeated. You give up and crawl back under the heavy rock of self-doubts.

Listen up, my fellow Leader. *The real problem is that you're not consciously deciding WHO you are!* Again, it's not outside of you — it's all a game anyway! **You get to BE who you DECIDE to be** — aka your Future Identity. Learning how to embrace your God-given uniqueness and anchor your Soul Design is a game changer that makes this whole market positioning thing EASY!

Take a deep breath … and let go … of the need to become someone else.

Using my methodology, you'll embody your Future Identity and realize that you are already the person you were meant to be by your Soul Design, and your people are waiting for you. All you need to do is be the one who connects the dots for them and shows them why you are the one they should choose.

And here's the best part: In Chapter 6 of this book, I will reveal how to leverage your uniqueness and forever free yourself from any competition. Your Soul Design makes you a one-time cosmic event, unlike anyone else in the world.

In fact, by implementing the techniques I share with you in this book, you'll be able to take your prospects from *"I'm not sure I get what you do"* to *"Holy sh*t, this is exactly what I need! Sign me up!"*

Ditch Bootstrapping Offers and Manifest One that Lights you Up

Let me tell you something about my clients who haven't embraced their Future Identity yet — they're grinding themselves down with the daily hustle, worshiping at the altar of busyness, and frantically trying to cross everything off their never-ending to-do lists. This is a recipe for burnout, frustration, and eventually, hating your business. No matter how successful you may seem, if you're always striving to get somewhere, you're stuck in scarcity mode and not truly thriving.

And let's be real, even the strongest and most rebellious of us can only keep going for so long without running out of fuel. That's why it's crucial to make a conscious decision ahead of time and fully embody your Future Identity. When you're already the person you were meant to be, success becomes inevitable and the grind fades away.

Let me guess — you've been hustling and grinding like a boss, but it feels like you're hitting a wall. You're no newbie to the game — you've tried every strategy under the sun, signed clients left and right, had successful launches, and even did lots of inner work to clear those pesky money blocks.

You are not new.

But what you are is *unhappy*. Despite all your efforts, you're feeling unfulfilled and close to burnout.

I hear you, and I'm here to tell you that there's a better way. See, *the key to unlocking massive wealth and success in your business is to tap into your Future Identity* — **that version of you who's already achieved everything you desire.**

And what does that version of you have?

She has an irresistible high-ticket offer that's aligned with your Soul Design, bringing you joy and fulfillment every step of the way.

Because here's the thing — you don't need to keep hustling and bootstrapping every offer, coming up with new freebies and classes every week. You don't need to launch a new thing every month either because you're bored or fear your audience will get bored. You don't need to sell yourself cheap fearing that no one will be able to afford the high-ticket.

I can hear you thinking:
- ❖ Can I let myself dream this much?
- ❖ Is it even possible to put into one offer EVERYTHING that I am about?
- ❖ Will this even sell?
- ❖ Would people pay for THAT?!

I'm here to simplify this for you — yes ☺

You can create ONE offer that encompasses everything you're about and sell it effortlessly, with ease and flow.

I know it might sound too good to be true but, believe me, — it's not. It's all about embodying that Future Identity of you who's already crushing it and designing an offer that aligns with that Vision.

Are you starting to see the light?

If you're constantly hustling and grinding, trying to prove yourself and accomplish your never-ending to-do list, you're not embodying your Future Identity. You're stuck in scarcity, always striving for something that's just out of reach. But when you decide ahead of time who you want to be, and you step into that identity fully, everything becomes effortless. The right clients show up, the sales come in naturally, and you get to live in the flow of abundance.

The secret sauce to creating massive Wealth in your business is to become the Future Identity that has already designed an irresistible high-ticket offer that aligns with your Soul Design and is selling it on repeat.

So, get ready to shine and stay tuned for Part 2 where I'll reveal all the juicy details on how to create your own Soul-Aligned Wealth Strategy — and especially that one amazing offer.

Stop Attracting Crunchy Clients by Saying the Magic Words

When you embody your Future Identity (based on your Soul Design Strategy of course), you tap into a level of confidence and power that can't be faked. You become the person who already has the success, the impact, and the income that you desire. And when you show up as her, you attract clients who are ready to invest in their transformation, who resonate with your message on a deep level.

But it's not just about attracting clients, it's about speaking to them in a way that truly resonates. When you embody your Future Identity, you intimately know your ideal client and can speak directly to the results they want. You know how to convey your message in a way that converts them into a "Hell yes, I need this, how do I sign up?" mentality.

Dear Leader, I know you're a total powerhouse in the coaching or healing world, with a unique gift for helping humanity elevate their consciousness and transform their lives in incredible ways. Whether you specialize in personal growth, relationships, energetics, leadership, ancestral healing, goddess empowerment, body healing, self-love, life purpose — whatever it is, it's all vital work, right?

We're living in a pivotal moment in human history, where many people are getting stuck in the illusions of the mind and emotions, mistaking conditioned responses for reality and becoming trapped in the Simulation. We're also facing extreme separation, where different perceptions are seen as absolute truths, causing people to lose touch with the inner truth of Maat. (Ancient Egyptian term for Divine Truth).

But here's the thing, my dear conscious Leader — this is the perfect opportunity for us to empower humanity to awaken and reclaim their power from those who seek to hold them back. You are here to lead the charge, to remind people of the importance of Maat, to empower them to disconnect from the fields of Separation and come together in the Universal family of Oneness. We are the ones who will shine the Light and guide people out of competition and toxic selfishness, into a higher consciousness of cooperation and service.

But here's the catch — if you focus solely on this message…

> … you'll only attract *"crunchy clients"* — the ones who want you to hold their hand every step of the way and complain about your prices.

That's why it's crucial to approach your message in a way that speaks to the heart of your ideal client — one who is ready to take action and invest in their transformation. That is what embodying this Future Identity is all about. **You BECOME her — the one who knows her ideal client intimately and speaks to the results that her client wants.**

So, dear Leader, to simplify your message so that it resonates with your soulmate clients and empowers them to reclaim their inner truth, you must step into that Future Identity that is pre-installed in your Soul Design.

Are you ready to lead the way?

It's time to unleash your inner badass and make a real impact!

In Part 3 of this book, I'll guide you through a set of specific steps to understand how to pick the most advantageous and aligned Future Identity and how to embody it as the key to achieving the success you were meant to have. But don't skip Part 2 — it will show you the actual steps to get there.

End Self-Sabotage and Become a Manifestation Master

Listen up, conscious Leader! If you want to kick self-sabotage to the curb and become a manifestation master, then constructing your Future Identity is absolutely critical. It's time to step up and become the person you were always meant to be — right here, right now! Don't wait for tomorrow, or next week, or next year. The time is now, and you've got this!

But first — let's talk blind spots! We all have them, even the most successful and badass Leaders out there. That's why we invest in coaches and mentors — to help us see what we can't. But here's the thing, personal growth isn't just about sipping green juice and doing yoga every morning (although those things are great too). It's about getting out of your comfort zone, taking action that scares the crap out of you, and unleashing your true potential. It's about being a warrior, a badass, a superhero goddess!

But let's be real, it ain't easy. It takes guts, resilience, and a willingness to face your own demons head-on. It means confronting your fears, healing your wounds, and becoming the best version of yourself.

And here's the juicy secret: the only way to do it is by tapping into your Future Self.

That's right, dear maverick. **You are going to have to become the person you want to be, NOW!**

Because without it, you're just going through the motions, playing small, and holding yourself back, no matter if you are clawing your way to 7-figures or struggling to get to your first $100k.

Let me break it down for you how *embodying your Future Identity simplifies it all:*

❖ Sabotage is always the resistance. It's you not being who you're meant to be, and not doing what you're meant to do.
❖ Aligned action, even if it scares the hell out of you, is ALWAYS the right choice. And when you do it with self-love and courage, that's when the magic happens.
❖ And finally, the only way to create ease, flow, and consistency in your biz is by BECOMING the Future You who already has all the things.

That's when you can make shit happen, without all the pressure and overwhelm.

In Part 2 I will show you specifics of what separates the conscious Leaders from the rest of the pack so you can embody your awesomeness, claim your power, and watch your business and finances skyrocket to multi-6 and even 7-figures. So go ahead, BE your own superhero. Face your fears and kick ass! You got this!

Self-Reflection for One Domino

Before we dive into the juicy content of the rest of this book, let's get real about where you're at right now in designing your Future

Identity and where you are with the five essential components of your business that are non-negotiable for reaching those multi-6 or 7-figure levels of success.

Do you have a clear picture of who must you become to consistently show up as the badass Leader of your successful business? Take a moment to reflect on where your identity currently is and jot down any insights that come up for you. It's important that you have these insights handy as we dive into the detailed content of Part 2 and 3 of this book.

Are you ready to become the manifestation master you were born to be?

Grab a pen and paper, because we're about to get honest with ourselves! Below, you'll find a series of statements that you'll rate yourself on a scale of 1 to 5: 1 being "not accurate at all" and 5 being "hell yeah, that's totally me!"

Once you've rated yourself on each statement, add up your scores and use the Answer Key to determine your next steps. Are you ready? Let's do this!

SELF-REFLECTION STATEMENT	RATING
My offers are positioned to evolve with me as I grow (without having to create new offers every time I leap to the next level of my evolution).	
I never believe my doubts and fears — I am kind to myself but I take aligned action despite them.	
I know whom I am meant to serve and speak to the most premium prospects in this category.	

I have a system or method, I am able to deliver my services without pressure, stress, or excessive customizing.	
I have no problem following through on my decisions no matter what emotional weather I might be having that day.	
I make decisions quickly enough, I don't procrastinate or spend energy on worrying about outcomes.	
I know my Future Identity and can easily embody it when speaking to my ideal clients.	
I am clear on the specific ways I am meant to create money and my sales strategy is built around this.	
I am crystal clear about which lead generation strategy suits me the best and costs me the least amount of energy.	
My business is directly built around my Soul Mission.	
I know exactly the ONE main problem I solve for my ideal client, a tangible result that can be measured.	
My clients have NO resistance paying my high-ticket prices.	
My sales calls are natural and comfortable, I know exactly what to say without having to "sell".	
My new prospects come to the sales call already desiring to work with me, I never have to prove I am trustworthy or capable of helping them.	
I do NOT lower my frequency when I feel negative emotions, my emotional baseline never sabotages my income.	
TOTAL UP YOUR SCORE >>>	

What your score really means (the Answer Key):

SCORE: 1-20
Your Complexity is Killing You

Oh, my dear rebel, I can sense that the current state of your business is leaving you feeling overwhelmed and confused. The complexity of it all may even have you switching niches frequently, struggling to sell your high-ticket offer, and lacking consistency in your delivery.

But let's not forget about your inner game! Your emotions and limiting beliefs are all over the place and it's hindering your ability to move forward. Your fears and doubts are causing you to question your own capabilities, leaving you exhausted and unable to create progress.

And that's why I'm so glad you're here, because stepping into the Future Self and manifesting correct-for-you Niche, Offer, and Message — well, that can change everything! This is not about "hope", it is about *certainty* that the power is right here at your fingertips.

What you truly need is to tap into your Future Identity to simplify it all, and master the art of decision-making and follow-through that comes out of it. By doing so, you can simplify your business strategy and create progress without any added pressure or stress.

I know you're ready to take that next step! Make sure to check out Chapter 9 in Part 3 about the inner game, and don't skip on anything in Part 2 of this book. Believe me, you won't regret it.

SCORE: 21-44
You Are Making It Too Hard

I sense that you have a lot on your plate and you're constantly hustling to learn and implement new business and marketing strategies. But despite all your efforts, you still haven't landed on something that feels right all the way. You get the thing to work, then something else happens and you are not sure anymore. You may be attracting clients, but not always the dream ones you truly desire.

You may also be struggling with payments, experiencing clients who back out or complain about your prices despite your great results. And even though you have a great offer, you're overworking yourself, there might be too much customizing going on, and we both know it's all underpriced. You've built your brand around your unique gifts, but this also locked you into the cycle of "only you can do this" and getting correct support feels impossible. It's like you've painted yourself into a corner, and you're not sure how to get out.

But don't worry, Leader, you can tap into the magic of your Soul Design to embody your Future Self and streamline your business — your Niche, your System, your clients, your sales process, your Message, and your marketing.

Take some time to review Chapter 7 — the parts on Expertise, Niches, and System. And make sure to pay extra attention to the parts on Message and Scale. Once you align your business with your Soul Design, everything will fall into place.

SCORE: 45+
Make One Degree Shifts to Scalability

I'm thrilled to see you here! It's evident that you know yourself and your business well enough to have an overall correct strategy and attract the right clients, even if you've fallen into it intuitively. And let's give credit where it's due — it takes a lot of self-discipline and courage to step out of your comfort zone and build a business from scratch. Kudos to you!

But I know that despite your hard work, some parts of your business are still not as scalable as they could be. Probably your prospect funneling process needs some tweaking, or your delivery is way too complicated. Perhaps you've been outsourcing the wrong things, having difficulty delegating, or trying to hold onto control by doing it all yourself. And let's not forget those emotional waves that can knock you down when you least expect it. It's a lot to handle, and you're probably wondering if it has to be this hard.

Well, it doesn't have to be! Now is the time to fine-tune your whole freaking business (and yourself!) so that everything is aligned with your Future Self and your Soul Design. This way, you can generate incredible momentum and make your business work for you.

Make sure to check out the rest of the book, and pay extra attention to Part 3, and the Scale Step #6 in Chapter 7 as well, they will be a game-changer for you!

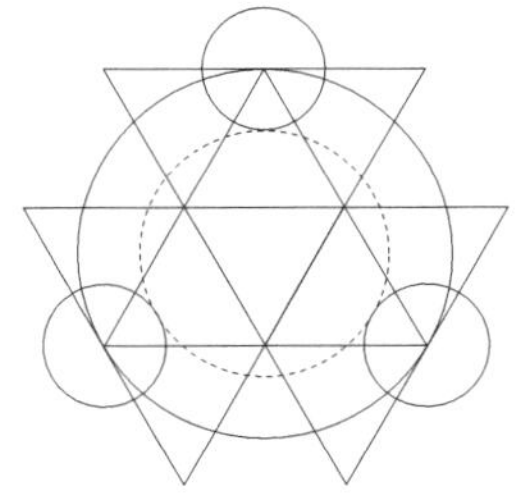

Chapter 5:

WHAT'S THE CATCH?
NO WAY TO 6+ FIGURES
FROM WHERE YOU ARE

"Fall seven times, stand up eight."

\- JAPANESE PROVERB

So, let me guess — you might be thinking, "Oh, all I have to do is tap into my Soul Design, become that imagined Future me, and everything will just fall into place, right?"

The business that scales is the business that can sustainably maintain discipline to keep selling no matter how YOU, the owner, feels. This is…

the missing piece of the puzzle that will allow you…

to create the success and impact you desire.

Let me break down for you the three big, bad misconceptions that coaches have when it comes to scaling their businesses to multi-6 or even 7-figures:

* Misconception #1: **Thinking that clearing up money blocks is the be-all and end-all.** Don't get me wrong, addressing those mindset hurdles is crucial, but it's just one piece of the puzzle. You need to take real, tangible action to make it rain, my friend.
* Misconception #2: **The whole "fake it till you make it" mantra.** Let me tell you something: success ain't built on a foundation of smoke and mirrors. You got to show up authentically, be true to yourself, and put in the work. No shortcuts, no pretending. When you embody your Future Identity, you're not faking it, you're authentically owning your badass power!
* Misconception #3: **Believing that the key to scaling is simply acquiring more clients.** Sure, clients are important, but it's not a magic fix. *If more clients are added to the broken system, it will only break faster* (and break you in the process!)

It's frustrating, I know. Like hitting a brick wall when you've followed all the instructions from your coaches or courses, but still find yourself stuck in a broken system.

Here's the truth: *magnifying a flawed foundation only makes the leaks gush even faster.* And to make matters worse, our own fears, doubts, and insecurities come creeping in, sabotaging your progress, even when we know exactly what needs to be done.

I see you, amazing woman, with your big heart and the burning desire to make a conscious difference in this world. But somehow, you end up feeling stuck and burnt out. I bet you've been caught in this vicious cycle before: that inner dilemma of pushing through, thinking, "I have to get this done, then I can finally relax." But deep down, you know that pushing too hard will only cause harm. It feels like re-wounding yourself, and you're wise enough to know better. So, you try a different approach, connecting with your heart and accepting yourself lovingly. Yet, in the process, nothing seems to get done. Now you're stressed, overwhelmed, and feeling even worse!

No wonder it just didn't click for you before. *You were missing a crucial puzzle piece*, but don't worry, I've got you covered!

Frantic hustle and emotional wobbles are not scalable.

Let me tell you, Leader, you're not alone in this struggle. It's time to break free from this cycle that keeps you spinning in circles. You deserve a better way. Scaling your business and making a difference doesn't have to come at the cost of your well-being and sanity.

My method naturally helps you empower yourself to become the fierce, unstoppable version of you. The one who doesn't need to override her own instincts, but effortlessly follows through with grace and determination.

See, it's that pesky *friction*, those internal indecision and wobbles, that make everything feel so damn difficult! Just like in the client case studies I've shared with you earlier — the friction was killing them.

Here's the kicker: we don't just slap a spiritual band-aid on the issue. Oh no, *we dive deep and get to the root of the problem*. It's all about *addressing the resistance within you*, dear Leader. It's about fully embracing and embodying the person who already has what she desires. That's where the real magic happens.

Now, in Part 3, I'll spill the tea on non-linear Quantum Creation and why it's the bomb. But before we get there, let's talk about *what truly enables you to step into your correct Future Identity.* The one that's beautifully aligned with your Soul Design Strategy, ready to soar to those magical heights.

Drumroll, please!

The key missing component is none other than **Soul Discipline**.

You've got to implement what I call *Seven Sacred Rules.* These bad boys are the secret sauce to unlocking your full potential. (Don't worry, I'll let you in on all the juicy details in Part 2, Chapter 8.)

I feel you! You're doing all the spiritual things, journaling, meditating, visualizing like a champ. But when life throws you a curveball, it feels like you're just crumbling under the pressure, am I right?

That's why I'm here to tell you that *true self-mastery is not just about having spiritual knowledge, sensitivity, and awareness. It's about having the discipline, the true grit, to commit and take aligned action towards your goals.*

Being self-masterful means gracefully navigating life's challenges while staying laser-focused on your vision and consistently taking action towards it. It's not just about tuning into the Light and hoping for some magical manifestation (and money!).

It's about taking that spiritual knowledge and applying it to your everyday life and business. It's about actually manifesting that freaking thing you desire! Sure, you'll face periods of darkness along the way, but your business doesn't have to be sabotaged by them.

If you're ready to unlock the full potential of your Soul Design, and stop the endless clearing of money-blocks, faking it, or forever chasing after "more clients" — you've got to powerfully show up with Soul Discipline and unwavering commitment to your Vision (the *Seven Sacred Rules*) — *so you can take aligned action towards your goals despite ANY external circumstances or internal wobbles.*

So, that's where my **Seven Sacred Rules** come into play.

First, let's set the record straight and debunk some misconceptions about discipline. See, most people have this faulty mistranslation in their minds. They interpret discipline as something being done to them, like they're being forced or punished. It's like that inner child within you, the younger part, feels resistant and rebels against doing something you don't want to do.

Can you relate?

But here's the thing, Leader: when your business strategy is sourced in your energetics, your Soul memories, and even your very DNA, a whole new world opens up. It's not about feeling forced or resistant anymore. It's about stepping into your power and fearlessly showing up to do what is necessary. That's when you're truly creating *Wealth by Soul Design*.

And guess what? It feels easeful, natural, and oh-so-aligned.

You do what you have to do, even when it's challenging or not exactly what every part of you desires. But here's the beautiful part: *you no longer leak energy in the process.* The friction that used to weigh you down is reduced, or better yet, eliminated altogether.

This is the true essence of being *free and wealthy*, Soul Sister, and let's debunk some misconceptions while we're at it:

Freedom isn't about doing whatever you want whenever you want, as many people believe.

Wealth isn't merely measured by the amount of money you have in your bank account.

Freedom is about owning your *will* and having the ability to make decisions towards your Vision. It's about **prioritizing long-term gains over short-term distractions**. It's about embodying the power to shape your destiny and create a life that reflects your deepest desires.

When you're fully aligned and 100% committed to your Seven Sacred Rules, magic happens. *There's no friction holding you back anymore.* Instead, you unlock the abundant wealth that your Soul has in store for you.

And here's the magical secret: when you master yourself, everything has a chance to be mastered with ease.

Instead of overthinking and chasing tactics or leads, you now are able to generate a sustainable energy that radiates clarity in your Niche and Message. It fuels your Sales and allows you to deliver your Offers with passion and authenticity.

Everything else is an add-on.

So, if you are struggling with your niche, your high-ticket offer, and growing your coaching or healing business to match your Vision, that's because you're not following the Rules of Soul Discipline. And without stellar Soul discipline, you'll continue to experience roadblocks and detours.

> When you have Soul discipline, you show up for your Vision, confronting your fears and doubts head-on, and gracefully moving past them with kindness.

> You get to be choosy about what you sell and who you work with.

And once you harnessed that discipline, you get to Quantum leap your Soul Mission business into the premium market. It's a journey that leads to financial freedom and grounded certainty, the very essence of your wildest dreams.

This is why the Soul Discipline and application of these Rules religiously into your life is the secret sauce that allows you to create amazing success.

We'll dive deeper into that later in the book (specifically in Chapters 8 and 10), explore the depths of Soul Discipline and the Seven Sacred Rules.

In the next chapter, we'll explore the entire Conscious F.U.T.U.R.E. Method — the system for turning a busy awesome coach or healer like you into a high-ticket magnet that lives her Soul Mission without friction. It is a unique combination of solid business strategies to help you elevate to the premium market and sell high-ticket, and non-linear Quantum Creation that creates shortcuts to your most lucrative timeline.

I won't sugarcoat it and promise you a journey of sheer ease, for we both know that building a business requires effort. If you get nothing else from this book, please remember that ANY tactic by itself is no help to scaling your business. You need a system that can leverage your Soul Design badass magic, paired with non-linear Quantum creation, activated by the Soul Discipline so you can handle yourself and be able to maintain the focus to finally get to these 6, multi-6, or even 7-figures. Without friction!

Ready to dive into the exact system we use — the Conscious F.U.T.U.R.E. Method — and scale in alignment to your Soul Design Strategy? Part 2 awaits!

KEY POINTS FOR PART 1

Why it feels so hard. The main reason why your business feels so hard is not the actions you are taking, but the energy of friction that is wrapped around these actions. You don't have to "work hard" to achieve success. You do have to be dedicated and committed, able to efficiently push and hustle for a sprint when needed, but not for a marathon. The more you follow through on your decisions, and the more in flow you are, the easier everything becomes. This includes attracting high-paying clients and creating abundance in all areas of your life.

Why proven Business Strategies don't seem to always work for you. Cookie-cutter strategies lead to forcing yourself into doing something that doesn't fit you because *it's not customized*. You might have short term success but feel trapped in doing business the way that feels wrong (or rebel and procrastinate). True success requires a fundamental shift in mindset and approach that is aligned with unique energetics of your Soul Design Strategy, with your purpose and values.

Why despite the best explanations about what you do (and being really good at doing it), no one outside of your circle gets what you're saying. The problem isn't that your offer isn't good or valuable, but that you haven't found the words to connect with your potential clients. Without *Soul Design aligned words*, you over-explain or don't use the language your clients can relate to. People don't care about the specifics of what you do; they care about how you can help them achieve their desired outcome or transformation.

Why are you Dreading these Sales Calls? You might have a mindset issue about the selling process. Limiting beliefs like feeling like you have to be pushy to make sales or guilt and trick people into buying hold you back from being highly visible online, attracting clients, and growing your business. When you're afraid to sell, you block the attraction of the clients you need to grow your business and increase your income. *When you are selling aligned to your Soul Design Strategy, it feels easy and natural.*

Where to find these high-ticket clients? The biggest misconception about finding high-ticket clients is that they are some special rich people. The truth is that high-ticket clients are "premium level people" with specific psychographics, and they exist in your audience already, you just haven't called them out yet. *When your messaging is on-point with your Soul Design Strategy, instead of chasing clients, convincing people to see the value in your work, or pressuring them to buy, they will be coming to you, already pre-sold, ready to make a decision.*

One domino to topple them all? To sustainably grow your Soul-led business to multi-6 or 7-figures, you need these *five components: clarity on your Soul Expertise superpowers, a unique methodology, a compelling high-ticket offer, perfect words to attract ideal clients, and emotional and energetic mastery.* The key to toppling ALL these struggles is a *Soul Design Strategy,* which I'll reveal in Part 2. It will give you room to breathe and easily elevate your business to the next level.

The Catch: No way to 6+ figures from where you are. The biggest misconception in scaling a coaching business is that you simply need to have more clients. But adding more clients to a broken system will only break it faster (and might break you with it). Frantic hustle and emotional wobbles are not scalable. Instead, the key is Soul Discipline (and Seven Sacred Rules, addressed further in Chapter 8 and 10), facing the resistance within you and fully embodying the person who already has what she desires. You do what you have to (even if it is hard at times), but you do NOT leak energy anymore. The friction is reduced or eliminated.

Part 2:

My 6-Step Process for Building a Multi-6 or 7-Figure Soul-Led Business That You Love

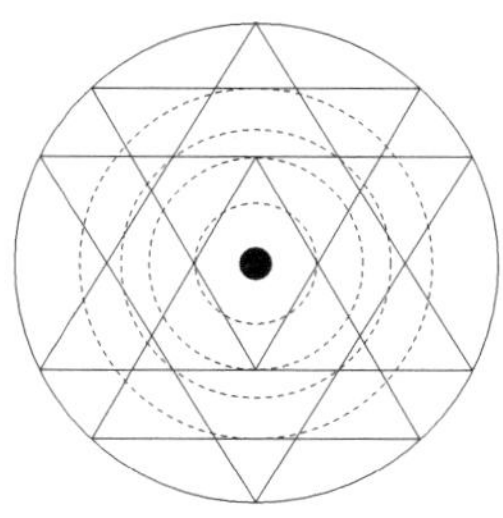

Chapter 6:

THE SECRET NAVIGATION KEY

"I am she who rises like the Sun, setting a flame in my heart: I am the Unique One."

- NEFERTITI, THE QUEEN OF EGYPT, 18TH DYNASTY, 1337 BC

As we dive into the 6 components of my **Conscious F.U.T.U.R.E. Method** that will help you grow your business in a Soul-led way, and scale into multi-6 or 7-figures without having to force yourself into unnatural-for-you strategies, let's start by unlocking **the secret key to your success: your Soul Design Strategy**. This internal map will help you leverage your unique badass inner magic and finally let go of the pressure and friction in your business.

Even if right now you are already succeeding and doing mostly what you love, chances are you want to add fuel to that fire and scale, right? By clarifying your Soul Design, you'll gain the secret navigation key to avoiding burnout and stop forcing yourself into strategies that don't align with your true self.

While there are numerous methods to discover your Soul Design Strategy, my unique process of determining clients' Soul Design Strategy combines my own clairvoyant insight and multi-dimensional access with tools like the Akashic Records, Transformational Psychology, I-Ching, Quantum Human Design, Wealth Energetics, Gene Keys, and Archetypes.

Your Soul Design Strategy is crucial to your business success as it fits into your Business Energetics and determines your Profit Potential, Branding, Purpose and Mission, Unique Superpowers, and Messaging. By navigating and embodying all of these aspects authentically, you become a magnet for high-ticket clients because your energy is vibrating at a premium level, and your confidence in what you offer becomes unwavering.

The simplest way to do this is by *uncovering your Archetypes*, the universal way the human collective organizes personal story patterns. We'll integrate their magic throughout the forthcoming chapters to help you gain clarity on your Soul Design, your Expertise, your Soul Niche, and countless other aspects of your business.

Get ready to experience an **epic bonus** that will blow your mind! Within this book is *the opportunity to uncover your very own two Archetypes*. Read on!

Your Archetypes are a shortcut to your Soul Design Strategy, and when you embody them, then you're living and breathing your true purpose, that's when it feels magical. Your message becomes crystal clear and converts well, your confidence skyrockets, and *you're not just doing what you can do, you're doing what you were BORN to do*. That's when you stop playing small and unleash the ultimate version of YOU!

So, what are these Archetypes?

They are the way that the human collective organizes personal story patterns. When your Soul incarnates on Earth, it has a specific contract that is a combination of gifts and lessons that you are meant to experience in this lifetime. To activate your gifts and learn your lessons in the most efficient way, your Soul utilizes the pre-existent parameters of this Simulation. These parameters can be thought of as Archetypes — an energetic range or collective pattern that is pre-set inside the Simulation. The linear laws of physics only apply within this 3D Simulation — beyond it there are completely different rules of non-linear Quantum Creation (which I will teach you how to navigate in Chapter 9).

There are 12 Archetypes divided into 4 quadrants: Mastery, Authority, Sovereignty, and Love. Each Archetype has its own unique strengths and characteristics.

- ❖ Mastery: Sage, Artist, Explorer
- ❖ Authority: Alchemist, Maverick, Jester
- ❖ Sovereignty: Ruler, Hero, Humanitarian
- ❖ Love: Innocent, Romantic, Nurturer

While this book is too short to cover my entire Soul Design Strategy system, don't worry. In this Chapter, I'll provide a starting point for you to uncover your Archetypes and other parts of your Soul Design Strategy, which you can integrate into your business and branding to create a powerful, authentic, and aligned presence that resonates with your ideal clients.

Here's your bonus: I invite you to click on the link to access the ARCHETYPE ASSESSMENT: eugeniaoganova.com/archetypes

Once you've completed the assessment, *return to this very spot*, for we shall weave the magic of your Archetypes throughout the forthcoming chapters to gain clarity on your Soul Design, your Expertise, your Soul Niche, and countless other aspects of your business. So, without further ado, go forth and embark on the assessment of a lifetime. I'll wait.

Did you do it?

No?! Go do it right now — you'll need the information to get the most out of the next pages (it'll only take 5 minutes and a piece of paper if you don't want to print it out).

***

Let me give you an example about myself to show you how easy and fascinating discovering your Archetypes can be.

As a *Ruler and Explorer*, I am here to empower my clients and build financial empires (Ruler) by exploring the possibilities beyond their current limitations (Explorer). This gives me the confidence and trustworthiness that sets my market positioning as someone who works with the pioneers of consciousness, leaders, coaches, and healers (Explorer). My message is full of Vision and Mission, both mine and my clients' (Ruler). I never go after prospects — I radiate my brilliance and strategically present myself so they come to me (Ruler), and on the sales call, we explore the possible timelines and visions of the future (Explorer).

By embodying both the Ruler and Explorer Archetypes, I become a Sovereign Master. This is Wealth Energetics that maximizes my Profit Potential. And the best part is, once you discover your own Archetypes, you too can effortlessly embody them and attract Wealth by your Soul Design.

Discovering your Archetypes also shows you who you should not be. For example, if I try to be a Nurturer (and opposite of Ruler), it will sabotage my ability to generate wealth and won't help the people who contracted with me on a Soul level.

***

Let's take a closer look at another example, let's call her Rose.

Rose is an *Alchemist and Nurturer*, which means that she is here to help people's dreams come true and catalyze her clients into awakening their hidden potential (Alchemist), while also providing them with a safe and supportive space (Nurturer). By balancing the magical and practical aspects of her work (Alchemist), Rose positions herself as a coach who works with people who have experienced trauma and need healing, someone who is unconventional and mindful of their specific sensitivities (Nurturer). Her message is filled with intuition that leads to deep transformation (Alchemist), combined with a sense of compassion and care for her clients' well-being (Nurturer). When it comes to lead generation, Rose offers support and value first, attracting prospects through her caring nature (Nurturer), and then helps them tap into their inner magic during the sales call (Alchemist).

By embodying her two Archetypes, Rose becomes a Loving Authority or Authoritative Love, which is her unique Wealth Energetics for her Profit Potential. As long as she embodies this frequency, she will attract Wealth by her Soul Design. However, if Rose were to try to embody the Ruler Archetype instead, showing up always polished, eloquent, and confident, she would push away the people she is meant to work with and make herself work very hard doing something that feels unnatural to her.

This is why it is crucial to understand your Soul Design and work with it, rather than trying to embody someone else's Archetypes and creating friction and hardship for yourself.

***

My program uses over 20 different tools to provide highly precise and targeted customization for you, and Archetypes are just one of the ways. It's amazing how everything else falls into place once you embody your Archetypes.

If you would like help in figuring out ALL of the aspects of your Soul Design Strategy and implementing them directly into your business, marketing, and messaging, that's exactly what my team and I do all day long.

If you're interested in working with us, don't hesitate to book a call to chat and see if one of our programs fits your needs. Visit eugeniaoganova.com/start to set up the Soul Strategy call.

We offer multiple services to help you accomplish every single step listed in this book.

In Chapter 7, I'm taking you on a deep dive into the practical side of my methodology for setting your business up for sustainable flow. Here, we'll look at how to break down your vision into achievable milestones and create systems that help move you closer to those objectives. It's time to take control of your success and unlock your full potential! Read on!

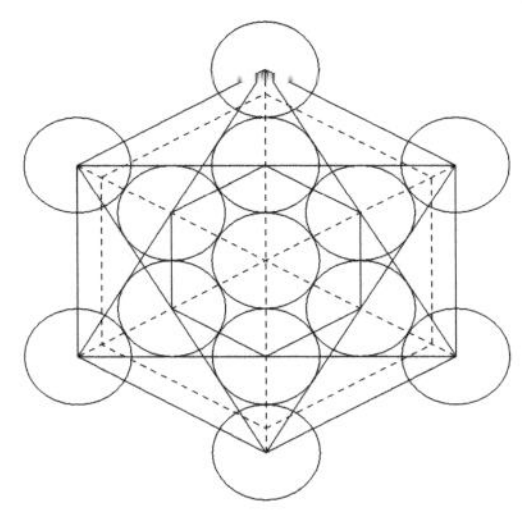

Chapter 7:

THE CONSCIOUS F.U.T.U.R.E. METHOD

"It had long since come to my attention that people of accomplishment rarely sat back and let things happen to them. They went out and happened to things."

- LEONARDO DA VINCI, 15TH CENTURY AD

In this Chapter, we will dive into the methodology itself. I will show you how you can go from a low-end stressful healing/coaching hustle to a simplified high-ticket business aligned with your unique Soul Design Strategy and positioned to sustainably grow to multi-6 and 7-figures without having to work harder.

At the end of the day, there are several key elements that drive a successful and sustainable spiritual business:

❖ Have you taken the time to get clear on your Soul Design Strategy, including your Archetypes and Expertise?

❖ Are you offering a Soul-aligned high-ticket Offer that fits seamlessly into your overall business strategy?
❖ Is your market positioning, messaging, and copy based on your unique Soul Expertise and Archetypes?
❖ Are you consistently visible online and actively promoting and selling every day?
❖ Do you have a no-hustle approach that includes both personal time for intention-setting, journaling, creating, and content-writing, as well as a supportive team and effective automations in place to ensure your success?

Once you have these foundational elements in place, everything else about the process becomes a matter of decision and follow-through. *It's no longer about random or frantic pushing, but rather about deliberate and efficient targeted effort towards your Vision.* And with the right help and guidance along the way, you can achieve your goals, build a thriving spiritual business and scale it into multi-6 or 7-figures!

STEP 1: Fuel Your Soul Design Strategy

We start by uncovering your unique Soul Design and integrating it into your business for sustainable momentum and flow. This is where we dive deep into the essence of who you are at the Soul level, your inherent energetic patterns that guide your thoughts, actions, and behaviors. *We extract your unique Expertise from your Archetypes.*

This naturally frees you from overwhelm, hustle, and resistance because you are unapologetically claiming your badass inner magic. By tapping into your Soul Design, you unleash a power within you that is authentic, aligned, and unstoppable. You no longer have to chase after success or force yourself to fit into a certain mold. You become the embodiment of your Soul Expertise and attract success effortlessly. You show up as your true self, and that's when the real magic happens.

You then can embody your Archetypes and Soul Expertise, you stand out as a "market of one" and attract clients you're born to serve — that is your Soul Niche. You have a unique blend of talents, skills, and energy that nobody else in the world possesses. You no longer have to compete with others because there is nobody else like you. You become the go-to person in your field and a magnet for clients and opportunities.

You have probably gotten by now that your Soul Expertise is already within you, pre-installed in your Soul Design Strategy. It's NOT a learned skill, but an innate ability that you came into this world with. It's so natural to you that you might not even realize how valuable it is.

Chapter 6 and your Archetypes Assessment explored your Archetypes in detail, and by now you should have a good grasp of your primary and supporting archetypes. By understanding these archetypes, along with a few other pieces I'll show you, you can gain a deeper clarity on your Soul Expertise and how it can drive your business forward. And believe me, this is a game-changer.

***

Let me give you an example. Imagine you're a nutritionist, and you've created a program that tells your clients how to get their diet balanced and live healthy, and you want it to sell for $5k. You're promoting it everywhere, but you're not getting many bites. So, you push harder, you add more things to your program thinking it will become more attractive this way. You're even hiring agencies to make your sales page and run ads, but it's still not working well — you get some sales calls, but most prospects are the wrong people. You're starting to doubt yourself and wonder if you're cut out for entrepreneurship and why is this so hard?

But here's the thing: you're NOT selling your Soul Expertise!

Let's say you're a Romantic Sage, a Love Master who's great at deepening intimate connections and finding specialness (Romantic), while also having incredible insight and wisdom and backing it up with research (Sage).

If you shift your program's emphasis to building intimate connections with your clients' bodies, creating a highly customized approach for each individual (Romantic), and write your sales page from the viewpoint of your personal insights and discoveries backed by research (Sage), you'll start attracting the right people — the ones you'll love working with!

FYI, in a few paragraphs I'll have a little exercise for you on how to get to know your Archetype a bit more deeply. So, remember, the difference between selling your skill and your Soul Expertise can make all the difference in your business!

****

You know what's crazy? So many entrepreneurs out there are selling their skills instead of their innate Soul Expertise! Let me give you another example.

Let's say you studied to be a life coach because you wanted to transform people's consciousness. You got certified, followed the templates on how to promote and sell your services, and charged per hour for life coaching. But you were bored out of your mind! You found it hard to find clients and people were asking for things that weren't aligned with what you wanted to offer. So, you studied energy healing, sound therapy, and tapping to keep yourself occupied. You realized there's a better way to serve your clients — by creating a longer-term offer. You built a course on energy healing for past traumas and living your best life for $1500, but it just didn't sell very well. You over-customized and wondered why it was so freaking hard.

Now, let's say you're a Hero Alchemist. That means you're a Sovereign Authority with a natural expertise in courageously facing pain, triumphing over adversity, and upholding worth (Hero) while bridging the magical and practical to make dreams come true (Alchemist).

You need to shift your focus to selling empowerment, courage, and triumphing over pain (Hero) paired with magical solutions (Alchemist) instead of life coaching or trauma healing (which is more Nurturer). Your offer should be something like "Discover the hidden meaning in your life lessons and leverage this wisdom for success". This way, you'll attract clients who are perfect for you and feel like you're just being yourself.

See how your Soul Expertise can make all the difference?

When it comes to truly standing out in the marketplace, you've got to tap into the power of your unique Archetypes. It's not enough to just think about them or analyze them from a distance. No, to really make them work for you, you've got to *embody* them on a deep, visceral level. That means imagining yourself as the embodiment of each Archetype, fully embracing its energy and making it a part of your being. Think of it like a *method actor* getting lost in their role — you want to immerse yourself in the Archetype so completely that you become it. When you do this, you'll unlock a whole new level of Wealth Energetics that can propel you to success beyond your wildest dreams.

***

You and your journal will become dear friends in the upcoming pages — get a cup of tea, your journal and pen, get yourself situated and ready to dive into self-exploration. This is not some flimsy task of writing down generic statements, superficial one-word answers, or half-hearted responses. **You get back what you put in.** Thus, dear Leader, allow yourself to truly investigate who you are. It is important that you don't skip this part because the more self-assessing you do here, the more clarity you'll have on your Soul Design Strategy.

In this chapter, we'll build upon the beautiful insights you've probably already written down as you read through the previous chapters, and ignite powerful inner shifts and awakenings. You know how it goes — a single realization has the power to catapult you into a whole new realm of existence. So, seize this opportunity and write with unabashed honesty, even if the answers aren't crystal clear just yet. Embrace the magic of this process with grace, and watch as your truth unfolds in glorious alchemy.

Remember the Archetype Assessment you took — what were your 2 main Archetypes? **Here are some journaling prompts to help your Archetypes and you become better acquainted,** so let's look into your true Soul nature this lifetime:

Can you feel the power of your *Primary Archetype* flowing through you? This is the energy that will propel you forward on your path to greatness, and it's time to fully embrace it!

* Close your eyes and feel the vibration of this Archetype within your body. What does it feel like?
* Which aspects of this Archetype are already shining through in your life and business?
* Are there any aspects of this Archetype that you find challenging to fully embody?
* Can you imagine how unstoppable you would be if you fully mentally embraced and emotionally embodied this Archetype?
* What would your presentation to your ideal clients be? What words would you speak if you were Her?

Let's tap into the energy of your *Influencing Archetype*, the one that comes naturally to you and has already shaped who you are.

❖ Take a deep breath and tune in to the frequency of this Archetype within you. How does it make you feel?

❖ Which aspects of this Archetype do you effortlessly embody in your life and business?

❖ Are there any aspects of this Archetype that you struggle to fully integrate into your energy and actions?

❖ How would your life and business transform if you fully embodied this Archetype in all aspects of your being?

❖ How would you present yourself? What words would you speak to your clients if you were Her?

Close your eyes and imagine the frequencies of BOTH of your Archetypes working together.

❖ What does this powerful combination feel like in your body?

❖ Think of a symbol or image that represents this energy blend and use it as a shortcut to tap into this powerful frequency whenever you need it.

❖ What actions do you need to take in your life and business to fully embody this combined frequency?

Write down any adjustments you need to make in your presentation or messaging. This will help you see where you need to go and how you can get there.

Pause for a moment, my visionary friend, and let your thoughts dance with these potent questions. Envision the impact that harnessing the magnificent power of your primary and influencing

Archetypes will have on every facet of your business. Feel the surge of excitement as you explore how they will infuse your marketing with a captivating allure, how they will breathe life into your messaging, and how they will transform your sales process into an irresistible force. Can you sense the limitless potential that awaits you? Embrace the depths of this inquiry and let your imagination soar as you unlock the secrets that will reshape your entrepreneurial journey. Give yourself a moment — journal about this.

You're at a pivotal moment in discovering your Soul Expertise and its connection to your Archetypes. Remember that your expertise is something innate to you, your natural superpowers that you may have overlooked because they seem so commonplace to you. It's based on your desires, lessons, gifts, pains, and your journey up to this point in life.

Extract your Soul Expertise

We want to position everything in your business around the component of your Soul Design called Soul Expertise. It is the innate superpowers you brought into this lifetime that are meant to become an integral component of your Mission, and thus help your business skyrocket!

Imagine you and I are on a coaching call, and I'm about to take you on a deep dive to extract your Soul Expertise. *These twenty questions below are the same ones I ask my clients to help them uncover their unique gifts and talents.*

Get your journal, grab a pen, and let's take this journey together. As we explore these questions, remember to give yourself the uninterrupted time and space you need to truly contemplate and reflect. Answering the questions will give you the clarity you need later on in your messaging to sign these high-ticket clients ☺ We're looking for that inspired moment of awakening that ignites your inner fire and brings your Soul Expertise to life. So, take this seriously and let's make magic happen!

1. What do you love doing and what comes naturally to you?
2. What are you passionate about? What gets you excited and energized?
3. What major challenges have you faced in life (the really rock-your-world types)? How have you overcome them? What did you learn from those experiences?
4. What unique perspective or approach do you bring to the table?
5. What do others come to you for advice or support with?
6. What do you find yourself talking about most often?
7. What is the karmic lesson you're here to learn in this lifetime? What growth direction is it leading you in?
8. What can you now teach others because of learning this lesson?
9. What is a common theme or thread that runs through your life experiences and accomplishments?
10. What superpowers do you have? How do you stand out from others?
11. What impact do you want to have on the world? If you REALLY were that badass magical Leader you feel yourself to be, in all your glory, what would it be?
12. What do you value? What matters to you the most? What do you care about deeply?

13. How do your Archetypes fit into your life's lessons and powers? In which ways do you embody your Archetypes to express yourself in a way that feels authentic and aligned with your values? (Describe this in detail for each Archetype, and the combined frequency).

14. What do you stand for?

15. What do you want to be known for?

16. Envision the future you desire and what you want to experience. What kind of person do you want to become? What kind of life do you want to have? Write it all down in detail.

17. What legacy do you want to leave behind? What do you want to be remembered for?

18. Who are the people you care about the most? (Describe that person in every detail) What do you know and can do that only you can give them and they desperately need?

19. If you had unlimited time, resources, and support, what would you be doing with your life? What would your ideal day look like?

20. What would you do if you knew you couldn't fail? What risks would you take? What dreams would you pursue?

Take the time to reflect on these questions and let your answers guide you towards uncovering more of your Soul Expertise. You want to have at least a few journal pages of written answers as you deepen in. Go through them and highlight the key words. Remember, you are unique and have something valuable to offer to the world that is different than your learned skills.

Now, look back at your journal entries and from those reflections, complete the paragraph below to identify your Soul Expertise, start by combining all your positive aspects such as what you love doing and what comes naturally to you, your passions, your superpowers, and what others come to you for.

These are ______________, ______________, ______________, and ______________. Your most frequently discussed topic is ______________ because your top three values are ______________. Your primary and influencing archetypes are expressed as ______________, and you stand for ______________.

On the other hand, the difficult aspects that you've persevered through, your karmic lessons, and the pain you've endured also shape your Soul Expertise. Your karmic lesson for this lifetime is ______________, which has taught you ______________. You overcame the top three major challenges of your life, which are ______________, because of your qualities, beliefs, and actions that include ______________.

A common thread of accomplishments that runs through your life is ______________. You naturally educate others on ______________ because the biggest lesson you've learned is ______________, and your impact on the world is meant to be ______________. You stand out from others because of your unique superpowers, which are ______________. If you had unlimited time, resources, and support, you would be doing ______________. If you knew you couldn't fail, you would take risks and pursue your dreams of ______________.

After answering these questions and filling in the blanks, you will have a clear understanding of your Soul Expertise. By knowing all of this, you can position yourself in the market as a "market of one" and showcase your expertise.

***

Let's look at one possible example — we'll call her Kathryn.

Kathryn naturally is able to empower people, she is passionate about helping women, and her superpower is that she is a wealth of knowledge and able to see a shortcut to making their dreams come true. You can find her most often speaking about various possibilities and occasionally being annoyed about how people just don't dig deep enough to see the root of their issues.

Kathryn's top 3 values are "dream big", "new solutions to old problems", and "follow intuition". You can probably guess by now, Kathryn is an Alchemist Sage and thus brings forth Authoritative Mastery for this world. She lived through a life-threatening illness and a betrayal in marriage, both of which she survived using her belief in magic and ability to perform thorough research. Her karmic lessons are to balance her magical side with her logical thinking, and forgiveness. These could be traced as a common thread throughout her life. She naturally educated others on options that they might not be seeing, and in beliefs that opened up their magic. She stood out as a Wise Woman who was also highly practical and grounded. She cared deeply about women struggling inside loveless marriages.

When Kathryn came to me, she was doing energy healing for over 5 years, and was generating about $60k per year. But she was working with anyone who came along doing whatever they needed, and that was not only draining her, it was also making her feel unconfident — her Sage was over-researching and over-doing for each client, and she never felt like she was solid, despite great results. Meanwhile her Alchemist didn't get much room to play because most of her clients had severe medical situations or even terminal conditions, and all of it was exhausting.

Kathryn knew that if she could feel confident about her energy healing work in the way that made sense to her, she would speak more about it, and she believed this would bring the right people to her. The problem was — she didn't know what to say...

We looked at her Archetypes and Soul Expertise and it became clear that she needed to focus her healing efforts on providing energy healing for the broken hearts of women who were betrayed in marriage. This would resolve the problem of dealing with incurable health conditions, which is the basic level of energy clearing many people could provide, but what Kathryn had was unique and of a higher level.

She didn't know before how to market herself — it felt that she just cleaned sick people's energy and tried to love them through the process. Now she felt excited about speaking about heartbreak in marriage and the toll this has on the woman's physical state. As she went live on video on social networks, created free gifts about this, and sent emails, the correct clients came out of the woodwork!

Her business went from stressed and exhausting "energy clearing" to multi-6 figures empire in just 4 months. She ditched her part time job and went fully in — because she now knew she could FEEL good doing it.

Now use this on yourself — go fill out the blanks and write up a paragraph about yourself just like I did about Kathryn. This will give you a clear view of your situation and where course-correction might be needed.

Land in Your Soul Niche

Alright, dear Leader, let's *identify the specific type of individuals you have Soul contracts with to help in this lifetime. This is a unique approach to finding your Niche* that I use in my methodology; it taps into the wisdom of the Akashic Records and reveals patterns in your life. These are the same 10 questions I guide my clients through.

So, grab your journal again, get comfortable and let's explore some questions together. Don't hold back, write freely and allow your thoughts to flow onto the paper (don't self-edit). Once you're done, take a step back and look for the main highlights in your answers. This exercise will help you gain a clearer understanding of your ideal audience and who you're meant to serve.

1. Whose thought patterns and ways of life do you understand at a deep level?
2. Who do you share (or shared in the past and now outgrown) the most similarities with in terms of lifestyle and mindset?
3. Who are the people that you've always known you had answers for, even if they didn't ask for your help?
4. What environment are you intimately familiar with and know all the good, bad, and the ugly associated with it or experienced in it? (Examples: "highly chaotic childhood", "corporate culture", "abusive or empowering relationships", "struggles of business owners", "self-healing", "motherhood", "public speaking and networking", "startups", "corporate team management", "traveling job", "healthcare", "personal leadership", "sibling drama", "mental health", etc.)
5. Who are the people that you feel the most spiritually connected to? Who do you feel completely yourself around? Are you their leader or follower?
6. Who do you have a strong desire to help and uplift? Why?
7. What environment do you care about, or have been in for a long time, and know with absolute clarity what is wrong with it and what must be changed? (Examples: "were in corporate management, know exactly what they need to change", "grow up in a toxic family, know exactly how not to raise kids", "lived in spiritual circles, know exactly what is missing", etc.)

8. Which current or past environment has the most go-getters with a clear vision for advancement? What was it? (Examples: "better health", "promotion", "next level of leadership", "fulfilling relationship", "deeper connection with themselves", "confidence", "clarity on aligned choice of career", "understanding of their purpose", etc.)
9. In which environment have you seen people with the most financial abundance, even if not in a healthy way, who could afford high-end services and were not struggling in their lives?
10. Who do you feel the most confident in your ability to assist or guide towards transformation (if they asked you to)? Who seeks your advice most frequently?

Got it? Great, Let's put it together then, just like we did before.

Drawing from my intimate understanding of ____________ [specific environment] ____________, and the ____________ [specific mindset] ____________ paired with ____________ [specific issues] ____________ and ____________ [specific desires] ____________ in it, I am uniquely qualified to advise on or help with ____________ [specific area of expertise] ____________ because ____________ [specific reason why you're uniquely qualified].

My Soul Expertise is ____________, ____________, and ____________ [specific qualities]. I have a strong spiritual connection with ____________ [specific audience], passionate about offering ____________ [specific type of support/insight]. Within this ____________ [specific audience], people who could most afford my service are ____________ [specific group of people]. My Soul Expertise applies to these people as ____________ [specific way you can apply your expertise to them].

***

Remember Kathryn? Let's see how this corrects her Niche.

When she came to me, Kathryn had ended her corporate career, still keeping some hours part time, as she was practicing energy healing for over 5 years. She envisioned herself as someone who was financially supported by her Soul Work, and desired to let go of the part time corporate consulting.

In the very first week, drawing on Kathryn's intimate understanding of the corporate culture she'd spent the past 30 years in, we've adjusted her Niche. It was apparent that she knew how women in corporate high-level management thought and felt, and she personally hated it — this is why she left her career of 20+ years! What Kathryn didn't realize though, is that these very corporate ladies she worked with were perfect clients for her! She knew their troubles, issues, and desires. Many of these women were trying to balance career and marriage, and their marriage fell apart because of the demands of their jobs. Kathryn knew all of this intimately and was uniquely qualified to help them because of her own experiences and how she was able to rise above the difficulty. They were also at the financially secure level in their lives and could easily afford Kathryn's services.

Kathryn's expertise was her ability to see magical solutions to practical problems, while anchoring it all in the solid grounded strategies, and using forgiveness as the key component, which was one of her own personal lessons. High-level corporate women with broken hearts who also had some health problems as they were processing all that heart ache naturally became a perfect Niche that could afford her.

See how magical this could be?

Your Soul Design comes preloaded with personal lessons, superpowers, and energetic agreements with specific type of individuals, the ones who are eagerly waiting to receive your unique gifts.

Deciphering this frequency and becoming crystal clear on how to showcase your talents, who to target, and what to emphasize in your messaging, gives you an unmatched level of self-assurance.

This is where you start to embody your true worth — your Mission is no longer just a mental concept; it is a physical manifestation. This also resolves the inner friction of worrying about competition, which stems from the desire to measure up to others. You're trying to compare yourself to those who you see as successful or to some idea of yourself that you've put on a pedestal. But this cycle can only be broken by stepping out of it and realizing that you have everything you need within you.

After reading these pages, you now know many components of your Soul Design Strategy: your Archetypes and how they relate to the uniqueness of your Soul Expertise, and specific Soul Niche that is the most lucrative for you because these people are awaiting your wisdom.

By sourcing your power from your Soul Design, you can further uncover your natural uniqueness and use it to create a clear pathway for how you work with your clients. This unique Soul Niche that comes from your Soul Design sets you apart from everyone else and naturally positions you as a "market of one."

Key Takeaways from Step 1 of The Conscious F.U.T.U.R.E. Method:

❖ **Through the integration of Soul Design into your business, you unlock a harmonious flow of sustainable momentum while liberating yourself from overwhelm, hustle, and resistance.** Say goodbye to imposter syndrome and doubts about your ability to deliver results, as you confidently unleash your inner magic.

❖ **Embodying your Archetypes and Soul Expertise sets you apart as a "market of one," sustainably attracting the clients** you were destined to serve. As you speak from this authentic place, marketing and client-attraction become natural, magnetizing opportunities and propelling revenue growth to new heights.

❖ Soul Design gives you a unique approach to discovering your Niche, drawing from the wisdom of the Akashic Records and revealing intricate patterns in your life. **This distinctive method positions you in the most lucrative niche where high-ticket potential clients eagerly await your profound wisdom and expertise.**

STEP 2: Unveil Your Premium Offer

Are you ready for your premium offer? Your Signature Offer is the vehicle through which you manifest not just Wealth, but also the profound expression of your Mission.

Just as your body serves as a vessel for your magnificent Soul, your offer becomes the conduit through which your transformative magic flows into the world.

If you've already discovered a way of working with clients that yields remarkable results, that is truly fantastic! Our mission now is to infuse it with your authentic essence, branding it to reflect the radiance of your Soul Expertise, rooted in the wisdom of your Archetypes. This infusion, Soul sister, will amplify your uniqueness factor, setting you apart from the sea of sameness that permeates the business world.

For the sake of simplicity, let us assume that you are fully enamored with the idea of a high-ticket offer by now, which allows you to leverage your time and energy in the most exquisite manner, enabling you to dive deep with your clients while being richly compensated for your gifts. It is a win-win that dances harmoniously with the flow of abundance.

Now, dear Leader, together, we shall make four foundational decisions that will breathe life into your high-ticket offer (or help you build one!), shaping it into a vessel of Wealth and Service:

1. **Signature System:** Ah, this is where the magic unfolds! We shall craft a system that showcases your unique process that your clients won't get anywhere else.
2. **Length of the offer itself:** We shall explore the perfect duration, aligning it with the ebb and flow of your Soul Design Strategy.
3. **Infusion of your Soul Expertise:** Here we'll add the "secret source" to your offer, creating a potent elixir that defies ordinary conventions.
4. **Delivery of this offer:** We'll explore the most Soul-aligned manner in which to deliver this exquisite creation, ensuring it supports you as much as your clients.

Can you feel the excitement building within you? Time to explore each of these areas, unraveling the mystery and empowering you to make these decisions in the most Soul-led way, so you can create or uplevel your high-ticket offer, and Quantum leap into the premium timeline.

Decision #1: Signature System

Are you ready to unleash the power of your Signature System, magical badass Leader? This is the very essence of the transformative journey you guide your clients through, illuminating their path with your unique brand of magic.

But before we dive deeper, let's clean up the three common issues you might be facing:

1. *The Everything-and-the-Kitchen-Sink Dilemma:* Perhaps you've created an offer bursting at the seams with every possible element, overwhelming both you and your clients. This approach not only adds unnecessary stress, but it also hinders your marketing efforts, making you launch all the time, post 10 times per day on IG or dance on Tik-Tok, while getting "I don't get why do I need this?" or "let me think about it" on the sales calls. We need to simplify and streamline to unlock your true potential.

2. *The Undercharging Conundrum:* Maybe you've built your offer solely based on your skill set, but when your clients invest in your magic, you naturally go above and beyond. After all, you can't turn off the magic, right?! The problem here is that you're not being adequately compensated for the full extent of your transformative powers. We must align your pricing with the value you truly deliver.

3. *The Lack of Clarity Quandary:* Or perhaps you find yourself without a clear offer, simply catering to whatever clients bring up. My dear, this leads to over-customization, inefficiency, and ineffective marketing. It's time to anchor

yourself in a solid foundation, enabling you to showcase your expertise with clarity and purpose.

Don't worry, for *the Signature System holds the key to resolving all these challenges.* In fact, without it, selling high-ticket offers becomes an uphill battle in today's market. Low-ticket offers may suffice without a system, but if you desire to ascend to the realms of multi-6 or even 7-figures with ease and momentum, it is imperative to create a clear methodology for your business.

Embracing this system is your gateway to liberation from the hustle lifestyle that breeds burnout.

Time to make a decision. The Signature System is an absolute necessity. If you've attempted to clarify your method in the past but found yourself stuck, despite achieving remarkable results with your clients and embodying awe-inspiring brilliance in what you do, don't fret, I've got you. Together we'll really simplify this for you, and it will blow your mind!

The Signature System is an answer to this question:

> *What are the steps in between the final outcome when your client is done working with you and the initial stage they come to you at?*

To answer this question authentically, we must first gain clarity on what you do for your clients. Reflect upon the core transformation they experience and the grounded practical aspects that accompany this journey. The secret lies in providing what is necessary without overwhelming or falling short. In this chapter, we will focus on the larger components of your system, exploring the duration and your unique approach in the next step.

Ready to dig in?

Grab your journal and a pen. As we explore these six profound questions, allow your thoughts to flow freely. Remember, there is no need to hold back. Later you will highlight what stands out and uncover the essence of your unique system. Let us begin.

1. **What is the main internal or spiritual transformation your clients experience in your world?** Be specific. Envision the beautiful shifts that occur in your clients. Is it the embrace of their energy guides' presence? The ability to receive from the vast expanse of the Universe? Perhaps it is the powerful journey of self-love, the release from dramatic karmic entanglements, or the liberation from limiting beliefs and outdated contracts? Or did they release the burden of over-responsibility and feel free now? Write down the essence of this transformation you help them create.

2. **What is the practical transformation that takes place in your clients' lives when they work with you?** Be meticulous in your description, dear rebel. Can they now speak with unwavering confidence to their boss, finding the right words easily? Have they mastered the art of setting boundaries with their children, or in the workplace? Does their dating profile radiate irresistible magnetism and they were finally able to complete it and begin actually going on dates? Did they hire that much-needed team member with ease and confidence? Asked for promotion or raise, and got it? Lost 20 pounds? Capture the essence of these practical transformations, for they are the tangible manifestations of your divine magic.

3. **What transformation do you create WITHOUT having to work hard at it?** Something that feels totally natural to you, and you almost can't believe that you are getting paid for it? (or wish you were!) It is essential, Soul sister, to find these areas of your work that flow effortlessly and do not cost you any energy as you deliver them. This allows you to create exceptional results without compromising your own well-being.

4. **What is the overarching transformation that seamlessly emerges from your previous answers?** It is a harmonious symphony of the internal and external shifts your clients experience, blended with what is easy for you to deliver from your Soul Expertise. Try putting it into one sentence, this is the very essence of your work.

5. **What are the effective steps that lead your clients from their current state to the ultimate transformation they experience in your presence?** This is about getting crystal clear on the direct route, NOT the scenic one! We seek simplicity and clarity. Identify the key milestones along this transformative journey, keeping in mind that no more than six steps are ideal, with a minimum of three.

6. **Describe each step: from the initial stage where your clients first enter your world, to the radiant transformation that awaits them.** *Paint a vivid picture of their experience.* (like "Step 1: this is how they come to me", "Step last: this is what "transformed them" looks like"). We know each client is unique, but overall, they all go through a specific journey with you. Each step holds the specific component they need to arrive at the result.

Now take a moment to reflect on what you wrote. Let's weave them together. Summarize your system with confidence and conviction. Embrace the power of these words:

"The main internal transformation my clients experience in my world is _________________, anchored in the practical transformation of _________________. I feel confident in my ability to help my clients achieve _________________________. The overall transformation they undergo can be best described as _________________, and I guide them through this sacred journey in _____ transformative steps. These steps are: ____."

Dear Leader, this simple structure shall serve as the cornerstone of your converting offer, empowering you to sell with ease and grace. Embrace the profound magic that lies within you, for your destiny awaits.

Decision #2: Duration

Welcome to a *pivotal moment where we make a conscious decision about the length of time required for your clients to experience the transformative results they seek.* It might look like an insignificant thing to you, but you better believe it, this can make or break your sales and your sanity!

Darling, here's a truth that can set you free: the length of your high-end offer is shaped by your intuition, your Signature System, and your client's needs.

As we explore this, if I was doing a Soul Design Strategy assessment for you, I'd know what could be the best length, but here I invite you to trust your intuition and tap into your profound knowledge of your unique gifts yourself. Prepare your journal, for we shall dive into three vital questions that will guide us to the perfect answer. Ready? Let us begin.

1: What characteristics define your soulmate client, the one who aligns perfectly with the transformation you offer?

Reflect on the psychographic aspects that make them an ideal match for your work. List at least five characteristics that resonate with the Souls you are destined to serve.

2: Now explore the clients who have achieved extraordinary results while working with you.

Whether drawing from your current client base or utilizing the power of your imagination, describe the specific psychographic details that set them apart. What qualities do these clients possess that contribute to their exceptional outcomes compared to other clients? Capture the essence of their qualifications that serve as pre-requisites of getting great results with you.

3: What time do these ideal clients need to get the best result?

Do they need 6 weeks? Or 3-4 months? Or 6 months? Longer? It's time to determine the optimal duration for your clients to achieve the greatest results. What is the duration they truly need to flourish? If you did the previous exercise in the Decision #1 properly, you know the most direct path you are guiding them through, so this is not "all that I do" or "all I can teach them", this is "to get through my X steps, how long do they really need?")

Now, my dear visionary, the time has come to make a choice, to carve out the perfect length for your high-end offer. This will not only help you in messaging and sales but will also allow you to leverage your talents and sustainably scale. Trust your instincts, for they are the subconscious reflection of your Soul Design, align your system and intuition.

Decide now. We will build the rest on it.

My ideal high-end Offer will be __________ weeks/months long.

Now, if your current offer already matches the desired length, awesome! You have discovered a harmonious balance that needs no alteration.

Should you realize that your current offer needs an extension, don't worry. You have the power to make those adjustments as you are integrating your methodology into your offer. And now that you know what your System needs, this should be a no-brainer — you can trust the timeline and start marketing it at that length.

But here's the thing, I find that for most coaches, the journey unfolds in the opposite direction. Their offers, born from a desire to showcase their immense value, become overstuffed with every conceivable aspect they can deliver and thus are either too long, or can't fulfill the promise in the limited time provided. These coaches believe that by offering more, they will entice high-ticket sales. But instead, this always backfires, resulting in disappointment and missed opportunities.

Remember, the ideal length of an offer is an art form, dear Leader. It is a delicate dance between showcasing your unique system and your client's needs. Strip away the unnecessary layers and focus on what truly matters, distilling your offer to its purest essence. It is within this simplicity that the true power lies.

Let your system and intuition intertwine, trust that the perfect length will reveal itself, a testament to your mastery and your ability to craft an experience that transforms lives.

Decision #3: Secret Sauce

Ok, Leader, let's dive into *the heart of your offer and unveil the secret sauce that makes it absolutely freaking irresistible.* But first, let's address two common mistakes that coaches often make in this realm.

The first mistake is trying to sell the secret sauce as the entire value of their work, attempting to explain its vastness and complexity. This approach sabotages the sale because it becomes too ungrounded and lacks a practical outcome that potential clients can grasp and appreciate. We must remember that value is not solely derived from the ethereal; it must be rooted in tangible results and transformation, especially if you want to sell premium, as in $5k, $10k, $20k offers.

On the other hand, the second mistake involves ignoring your unique superpower and undervaluing it. This stems from the conditioning that tells you that you must work hard for something to be valuable. When your gifts come naturally, you tend to dismiss their significance. This mindset leads to a constant battle of proving your value and over-marketing yourself, while drowning in a sea of sameness.

Did this ring some bells for you?!

Now, let's revisit your Soul Expertise, which we explored earlier in Step 1. To make this practical, *think of it as the way you deliver transformation to your clients.*

Let me illustrate this with a couple of examples.

Imagine you possess a remarkable talent for healing relationships, and your secret weapon is the use of Angel divination cards. These cards hold power in all your sessions, but if you try to sell them as the main offering, no one will pay a premium for it. See?

On the other hand, suppose you excel at helping women lose weight by teaching them how to listen to their bodies' subtle communication. If you position this program only as "weight loss for women" and bombard them with testimonials, you'll struggle to stand out in the crowded market. However, if you highlight the unique approach of empowering women to communicate with their bodies as the key to their weight loss journey, now you have a program that practically sells itself.

Now, my dear, it's your turn to explore YOUR secret sauce. Take the time to journal and *clarify the key unique component you can permeate your offer with.* Remember, it's not a standalone step; it's something that enhances the entirety of your offer, amplifying its uniqueness and power.

Decision #4: Delivery

Time to uncover the secrets to creating a better, streamlined, and spacious delivery system for your premium Offer. But first, we must expand your energetic Wealth capacity, allowing your container to hold the abundance you seek.

* Are you making a conscious choice to create more space in your business?
* Do you believe that you can attract abundant sales and clients without constantly hustling?
* Do you choose a path where your efforts are focused, and no energy is wasted?

By fully owning the worth of your Mission and charging higher fees, you manifest your Vision. It's about understanding and embracing your inherent value, attracting clients who appreciate your work and are ready to invest in themselves. This is the path to a thriving and abundant business that aligns with your soul's purpose. Congruent delivery is the key, as it aligns with your natural Soul Design Strategy.

And guess what? This freedom and spaciousness are available to all Soul Designs when the correct strategy is implemented. You simply need to be open to tweaking and experimenting to find the perfect fit.

Fine-tuning your timeline, Signature System, and high-ticket Offer around your Soul Expertise and Archetypes is the process that streamlines your marketing, delivery, and profits into one harmonious path. It eliminates complexity and provides you with built-in sustainability. *The key is creating a premium offer that reflects your Soul Mission and Expertise.* We'll dive into this in Chapter 8, but for now, let's explore the delivery of the offer you've crafted.

The delivery of your offer is what determines the kind of experience you have in your life and business. When you still have a client inflow issue, you run into this problem: you over-customize everything for each client, working way harder than necessary. This often occurs when you don't have a Soul-aligned high-ticket Offer or a clear methodology to rely on.

On the other hand, if you're fully booked with imperfect or lower-end clients right now, your one-on-one offer is selling fine but underpriced and running you ragged, as with most of my clients before we began to work together, then the main 2 problems you run into are these:

❖ Either you are in rebellion about converting your one-on-one offer into a group offer because you're afraid the clients won't get the same results (which we know is simply the lack of clear methodology here to rely on!)

❖ Or you are already running a group program successfully, but doing it all yourself and over-giving on steroids, close to burnout and not sure how to scale this baby, right?

The solution depends on the level you're at, and it's a huge mistake to apply a one-size-fits-all approach. Using the wrong delivery structure at the wrong stage can ruin lives, reputations, confidence, and health. I want you to have the most incredible experience living your Soul Mission and delivering your gift while being fully resourced.

Here are 3 levels that you want to adhere to for the success of your delivery.

So grab your journal and take a moment to gain some serious clarity. Which level are you currently at? Jot down those specific areas that need your attention next, so you don't waste your efforts on the wrong delivery strategy. Create a crystal-clear roadmap for your delivery process, aligning it with your Soul Design. Remember, you're a force to be reckoned with! Let's find out where you are:

Level #1: If you're still relying on one-off sessions, it's time to create a private high-ticket offer. Sell and deliver this offer, collect testimonials, and showcase them on your social media and website. Each chapter in this book provides guidance on how to accomplish this. Your challenge is to work with clients you love one-on-one in a high-ticket setting. This can be achieved through weekly phone or video calls with some email or Voxer support, without the need for additional materials. Once you've sold enough of these offers and feel that you've outgrown them (usually around 10-20 clients), it's time to move on to level #2.

Level #2: If you're selling an offer and realizing that it isn't high-end enough, congratulations! This is the perfect time to implement everything we've covered in this book — your Archetypes, Expertise, Niche, and System — and raise your fees. Sell your enhanced one-on-one offer and collect amazing testimonials to showcase on your social media and website. Your challenge is to fully book yourself with these incredible one-on-one clients, preparing you for level #3.

Level #3: You're already selling a group offer, let's get real about the overwhelm that's been creeping up on you. It's time to make some powerful adjustments to your delivery. Here's what you need to consider:

1. **Duration:** How long is this offer running? Is it dragging on like a never-ending soap opera or does it end too abruptly, leaving your clients craving more without the next step ready? Fine-tune that duration and align it with the powerful transformation you bring.

2. **Pricing:** Is your pricing really reflecting the mind-blowing value and insane results your clients get from your offer? Take a hard look and adjust that pricing, positioning your offer as the premium, high-vibe experience it truly is. You're worth it!

3. **Systems:** Have you explored the magic of automation and pre-recorded content? It's time to streamline, simplify, and make your life easier. Prepare that pre-recorded content, utilize automation tools like the boss you are, and watch your delivery become a well-oiled machine. Less work, more impact—yes, please!

4. **Responsibility:** Now, darling, it's time for a reality check. How much of your clients' results are you carrying on your shoulders? You're a guide, not their personal savior. Strike that balance, make sure you're providing guidance while empowering your clients to take personal accountability for their own transformation.

5. **Support team:** This might be time to bring in some reinforcements. Are you feeling the weight of the world while being booked with great clients? Well, it's time to delegate. Consider hiring additional support coaches, experts, or a kickass virtual assistant to help you deliver and manage your program with ease. And always invite your non-physical support team to help! You deserve that support!

Did you journal some revelations? It's essential to not try to use the wrong strategy for your current business level. Get clear on which level you are at, and jot down what you must focus on so instead of having to *do all the things*, you know which one thing to do next.

***

Let's summarize all of this with an example to show you what this looks like in action — let's call our example client Meredith.

When she came into my world, Meredith struggled with creating her methodology. She was booked with lower-level clients for individual sessions and ran a year-long group program, but she had to keep the price very low because she couldn't sell it high-ticket despite her attempts. It clearly became apparent that her group offer was premium already, and that she was severely undercharging and over giving, leaving her stressed and overworked. Meredith was lacking any system whatsoever: she promoted services in inner purpose discovery, 7-ray energy healing, chakra cleansing, releasing scarcity contracts, goddess activation, somatic release, breathwork, DNA activations, and opening to the Universe. From all this soup, her prospects couldn't understand the incredible value of her work, and thus wouldn't pay premium for it. She had a dozen certifications in anything from tapping and breathwork, to energy healing techniques and trauma resolution. She listed all of this on her website — and to her surprise, this didn't help. From the time she was a little girl, she could always resonate with the 7 energy rays and felt them to be a guiding light on her life journey. Originally highly successful in corporate mid-level management, but after having spiritual awakening at the age of 40, she lost interest in her career. Her husband at the time believed she had lost her mind and they divorced, leaving her to raise a daughter on her own. She began to do healing work on the side. She worked all the time, spinning between her job, her child, and her healing practice, diluting herself into thinking that this is what spiritual service should look like, while secretly hating this scarcity lifestyle filled with a pointless career, client's drama, and tittering at the edge of burnout all the time. Then, the health crisis came, and she had to let *something* go — she quit her job.

First, we investigated Meredith's Archetypes and other components of her Soul Design Strategy — it came as no surprise that she was Alchemist and Ruler. She ran an efficient ship, juggling complex parts of the job, raising her child, and clients (Ruler) while bringing magic into the lives of everyone around her and making the impossible possible (Alchemist).

In just 2 weeks, we helped Meredith zero in on the most lucrative system and simplify her offer (and with it, all her marketing too!) We focused on the mid-level corporate women whose life struggles she knew well. We realized that her healing work helped them go from stressed with too many pots on the fire, juggling family, and career — to having space for self-care and putting their needs and desires forward and getting raises and promotions. We created a 5-step system of guiding her clients through this process, that naturally included most of what Meredith did, from breathwork to trauma healing, to self-love and empowerment. This is something she did already in her year-long program, but we went from a scenic path to a direct one.

Meredith also realized that it was taxing her energy too much to have each client in her field for a year, and with a more streamlined system, she wouldn't need such a long time anyway — so we shortened it: 5 steps in 5 months made much more sense now that the steps were defined. Meredith's secret sauce was her 7-ray healing energy, this became the unique key to the whole system. And last but not the least, we made her delivery way more efficient by creating pre-recorded content for each step of her system and putting every client into one group where Meredith got to focus on all of them as a group healing and coaching, plus answer questions that were unique to each client so everyone could feel highly supported. We raised the price for this program to match the actual value (which was about 6 times more than what she was previously charging).

Meredith breathed with relief — she could now easily explain the value of her work, she had a clear methodology and results, she had an easier way to deliver her work without being limited. Her marketing became very simple, and at the very first sales call, the person signed up and paid in full without any objections. Meredith cried as she almost couldn't believe how easy this could be. She let go of private one-off sessions completely because she was now funneling everyone into her group program, which involved one group video call per week. She still had to do the work and show up, stretch outside of her comfort zone and promote her offer, but there was no more friction.

In Part 3, I will reveal how you too can eliminate friction and create ease, even when faced with uncomfortable tasks. So stay tuned!

Key Takeaways from Step 2 of The Conscious F.U.T.U.R.E. Method:

❖ **Embracing a high-ticket offer model empowers you to maximize your time and energy,** immersing deeply with your clients while being generously compensated for your divine gifts. **By infusing it with your authentic essence and branding it to reflect your Soul Expertise rooted in the wisdom of your Archetypes, you effortlessly amplify your uniqueness, standing out amidst the sea of sameness.** Four foundational decisions pave the way for a highly converting offer.

- **Your Signature System encapsulates the very essence of the profound transformation you guide your clients through,** illuminating their path with your unparalleled brand of magic. It is the key to overcoming challenges such as overstuffing your offer, undercharging, or succumbing to clients' wishes rather than leading them. **Without it, selling high-ticket offers becomes an uphill battle in today's saturated market.**

- The length of your offer is skillfully shaped by your intuition, Signature System, and your clients' unique needs. **Striking the right length not only enhances your messaging and sales, but also allows you to leverage your talents and sustainably scale your business.**

- **Infusing your Soul Expertise into your offer acts as the "secret sauce" that makes it absolutely irresistible.** It is crucial to avoid the mistakes of selling the secret sauce as the sole value of your work or disregarding your unique superpower and undervaluing it. Clarity on your Soul Expertise frees you from the need to convince people to buy or constantly prove yourself, making the process of selling your high-ticket offer much smoother and more rewarding.

- Choosing the most Soul-aligned delivery method for your high-ticket offer ensures that it supports you as much as it benefits your clients. **Fine-tuning your timeline, Signature System, and high-ticket Offer around your Soul Expertise and Archetypes streamlines your marketing, delivery, and profitability onto one harmonious path. This eliminates complexity** and offers built-in sustainability, allowing you to thrive and make a profound impact with ease.

STEP 3: Transform into Vision-Based Sales

Listen up, dear powerhouse! Sales is all about unleashing your unapologetic ability to clearly articulate what you do and why those prospects of yours absolutely need it. Let's ditch the notion that you need some damn magic script or rely entirely on finding those mythical unicorn clients who never utter a single objection. It's time to unveil the truth!

Here's the deal: If you've done your due diligence in creating an awesome Methodology and executing a killer marketing strategy for your Offer, based on your Signature System, then the folks who slide into your Messenger conversations or hop on those sales calls should be mostly the right people. But hold up, even these perfect creatures might experience doubt or need a bit of reassurance and guidance from your badass self before they are ready to whip out their credit cards. It's part of the human game, don't give it a second thought.

I want you to know that everything I do is infused with both energetic and practical aspects. Why? Because I don't want you to settle for anything less than building a damn empire that's authentically aligned with who you are at your core. And let me tell you, Sales are no exception. The energetics have so much power in this game. It's what helps us magnetically draw in those perfect peeps and hit that sweet spot of Soul resonance during our interactions, leaving them craving to join our programs.

Sales, Soul Sister, is an art form that requires a combination of knowing what to do and say (that's the practical and linear side) and mastering how the hell to do it (that's the energetic and non-linear side). We blend the two like a master mixologist crafting the most intoxicating elixir of transformation.

Let's put to use the work you've done in your journal so far — implementing the steps of my methodology will help you achieve these 3 critical concepts below to unlock your sales power!

So, what do you need to sign clients successfully? *Here are the essential ingredients for an effective sales concoction:*

1. You need to clean up the psychological crap of outdated beliefs and energy blockages that might be in the way of receiving Wealth, so you can freely embody higher fees and not wobble energetically when playing with bigger numbers. It's time to claim your worth with unwavering conviction.

2. You need to get these practical ducks in a row! Do you have a method that's forged from the depths of your Soul Expertise? Can you articulate it clearly, succinctly, and irresistibly in just a minute if you had to? Is your Offer aligned with this powerful method and your authentic Soul Design Strategy? And let's not forget about your marketing game. Is it showcasing your *method* (or the logistics of your program that no one cares about)? Are you selling in your content every day in some way? Ensure that every piece of the puzzle is in place.

3. You need to know exactly what to say to show your clients that you are trustworthy and great at what you do, and able to lead them with power, clarity, and love. When you are in the correct energy, radiating the essence of a coach who is destined to guide and transform their lives, it's not just about the words you speak — it's about the confident energy you exude. Subconsciously, your potential clients will feel the magnetic pull, drawing them irresistibly towards you.

Alright, time to shift your Sales process from feeling overwhelmed, frustrated, or undervalued to being confident, clear, and aligned with your worth. Are you ready?

First things first, we need to address those pesky *limiting beliefs and energetic blockages* that might be holding you back from quoting higher fees and converting those leads into ecstatic buyers. To do this, I'll guide you through a series of the same 10 question-sets I ask my high-level clients, so get your journal, Soul Sister, and let's begin.

1. **Do you believe deep down that you must work very hard to bring money into your life?** Seriously, let's unpack this belief and see if it serves your highest good. Who programmed you this way? Is this what you stand for in your Soul? Why do you keep playing the "work hard" game? What negative benefit do you get out of it?

2. **Do you think that if you were truly deserving, you could charge higher fees?** How did you get to view yourself as unworthy? What do you get from seeing yourself that way?

3. **Are you caught up in the never-ending cycle of over-giving, people-pleasing, and tirelessly over-teaching in your marketing, for free, in an attempt to prove your worth?** How would you know you've finally proven yourself?

4. **Picture this: you're on a call with a potential client and they begin to wobble, they tell you that their issue is not that bad, it can wait, and they just need to wait for this or that before singing up with you... What do you do?** Do you believe their story and let them off the call? Do you think that if you dig deeper with them — you are manipulating them into buying from you? Do you see selling as convincing? Where did you get this belief from? Do you have the same standards as the person who is the originator of this belief? Or higher? Do you trust yourself to guide without coercing?

5. **Do you feel guilty or think it is greedy to charge premium fees for your service?** Like you're not being considerate and loving to people who can't afford you by excluding them? What would you think of yourself if you became highly exclusive in your marketing?

6. **Do you feel you need to sacrifice your authenticity or become someone-you're-not to generate multi-6 or 7-figures?** What kind of people are coaches who generate millions? What do you believe about them? In what ways do you judge them?

7. **Do you believe that high-ticket clients are scarce, and that attracting abundance is a constant struggle?** Do you feel you need to go into some special place where these high-ticket clients congregate to find them? Do you see yourself as not the type to hang out in such places?

8. **Do you feel that you must achieve some higher level of skill before you can charge higher fees?** Do you believe that getting more certifications will get you to be worthy of a higher price? Where did you get conditioned to think like that? What do you get from this limiting belief?

9. **Are you trapped in the cycle of people-pleasing, trying to be what others want you to be in order to secure higher fees?** Do you believe that giving them what they want or being who they need you to be will unlock their wallets?

10. **What do you believe would happen if you named a high fee, higher than you can imagine right now?** (It can be a $10k for a 6-month offer for you, or a $50k for 3 months, or $100k for 6 months — pick what would be super challenging and imagine that). Can you envision yourself confidently quoting that price? Notice what happens in your body as you explore this possibility. What beliefs get triggered? Will you faint? Will your voice quiver? Would you then immediately lower the number to please them? Will you feel happy and confident? Will you be immediately murdered by the prospect who is mad at you for your audacity? ☺

Journal extensively on these questions. They hold the key to revealing the underwater rocks that have been obstructing your path to abundance and prosperity.

Now, let's summarize the top three limiting beliefs that tend to pop up most often for my clients:

- ❖ Money is a proof of my worth, and I must work hard to earn it.
- ❖ I have to be special or extraordinary to charge higher fees, and I feel unworthy.
- ❖ Money comes from people, and I must constantly strive to earn it.

And here are the top three energetic blockages that typically come up:

- ❖ By charging premium I am hurting people, exclusion is wrong.
- ❖ Poverty is spiritual.
- ❖ I'll be ostracized, abandoned, killed for my audacity to value myself at that price level.

Setting those down once and for all, (as I hope you're learning to do so), here are the energetic truths that you can begin embracing **(you can use these as affirmations when needed!)**:

1. I am already infinitely worthy of all the Money in the Universe as I am being my Higher Self, aligned to my Soul Design.
2. Money is energy and it flows effortlessly to me through resonance, not hard work.
3. Money comes to me from the Universe, not from people, thus there is nothing to earn.
4. My Mission is fulfilled only when I narrow my focus to a specific frequency, being exclusive is what brings Money to me.

5. Abundance is divine and Money is spiritual, I can freely receive any amount I desire.
6. Valuing myself to charge aligned higher fees allows me to bring in more of my Wisdom and Truth and live my Purpose.
7. Curiosity about indecision leads to a decision.
8. Every situation is an opportunity to uplift me, bring abundance to me and others, and create healing.
9. I am always divinely guided to financial solutions and shortcuts to abundance.
10. Unreasonable courage to continue the journey vibrates higher than reason.

***

So far, we've covered the #1: limiting beliefs and energetics; and the #2: Expertise, System, Offer (in this Chapter 7, steps 1 and 2). Now, let's dive into #3: how to actually *sell*.

In a world where misconceptions about Sales have clouded the truth, it's time for a radical shift. Sales has long been misunderstood, tainted by the patriarchy's desire to manipulate the masses. But you, my conscious friend, have embarked on a personal awakening journey a long time ago. You understand that we are all connected as ONE, yet you also recognize that money plays an important role in this earthly game.

In the realm of eternal soulful abundance, where money is the energy that flows effortlessly, there must exist a process that allows Sales to feel absolutely fantastic, don't you agree? Let me share a secret with you: Every sales call I've ever had, whether or not the potential client decided to work with me, left them feeling immense value and overflowing gratitude for our conversation.

If you were a fly on the wall during my sales calls, you'd hear these three recurring themes when I inquire about my prospects' sales challenges.

- ❖ *"It's manipulative, they should just buy if they're the right fit."* This belief stems from limiting notions that blur soulful conversations with coercive tactics. Pressure exists only in guilt-focused sales fueled by immature masculine energy. But rest assured, done correctly, sales become a soulful journey that you and your potential client take together to discover if you are a good fit. Lead this process with integrity — this is where you want to help them get clarity to decide.

- ❖ *"I hate sales calls; and my DMs end up filled with free information seekers."* Oh, dear, the reason you despise sales calls is that you haven't mastered them yet! My clients not only enjoy sales calls, but they look forward to them. The secret lies in curiosity about your potential client and her indecision, embodying your Archetypes, and aligning your conversation with the essence of your Soul Design Strategy. Ask powerful questions, and if your marketing is on point (we'll discuss this in Step #4), your potential clients will expect that you'll introduce your paid offer on the call.

- ❖ *"Soulmate clients should come to me; I don't need to sell."* Ah, the illusion of waiting for the perfect clients to find you. While referrals can bring in clients, relying only on happenstance won't lead to scaling beyond six figures. If you're ready to reach for the millions, my dear, you need a strategy. Referrals are a delightful bonus, but *don't fall into the trap of spiritual bypassing and expect clients to magically flock to you.* Embrace the complexity of human nature and take intentional action.

Alright, dear magical badass Leader, let's dive into the world of Sales. Remember that Sales is a structure and an art, because you have to weave the words with the correct energy.

Have you ever found yourself winging it, unsure why your sales approach only works sporadically? Or perhaps you've been handed a rigid script that ignites a fiery rage within you. You may have reluctantly followed it anyway, only to discover that your energy refuses to align with the words. Alternatively, you might have been avoiding sales calls altogether due to this script-induced aversion.

And hey, maybe you're naturally gifted at conversations, and your sales calls don't feel like a horror show. But here's the thing: you probably tend to over-give, extending those calls to 90 minutes or even a whopping 2 hours! While your potential clients leave feeling elated, they don't always make that purchase.

Does any of this resonate with you?

In Step #4 we'll talk about incorporating Sales into your content. It's a must! But hold up, here we need to get your call-to-action (CTA) game on point. "Leave an emoji below if you're interested" just won't cut it. Your CTA should exude value and take up about one-third of your post or video. See, during that invitation, you're still providing your audience with immense value. Believe me, it's key!

But wait, there's more! You and your potential clients must meet within specific parameters that empower their decision-making. This is actually the very power of these sales calls — the fact that you get to set the Soul-aligned parameters for the sales process. Oh, and let's not forget about DMs, you can weave the magic of sales through messenger similar to the sales call. And obviously sales can occur in other ways: occasionally during a live event, or daily within your captivating content.

So, what is the proper structure for a Soul-led sales call? First let's define it. It is NOT about guilting, pressuring, or manipulating them to work with you. It is about helping them expand their perspective to see the real problem and you as the solution by becoming the Identity they aspire to embody.

I call this **Vision-based Sales**.

Get your journal and let's look into these components so that you can run your sales calls like a boss! Here's the breakdown:

1. Embrace your role as the leader: On the sales call, it's crucial for you to take charge and be the Leader. Set the parameters and declare the agenda right from the start. Make it known that you will explore x, y, and z during the call, and that the call will last for 45 minutes or whatever time you decide. Then, together, you will determine if you're a match to work together. Your leadership extends to guiding them towards a decision, not controlling their choice. This isn't about free coaching, though!

2. Strategic questioning vs solutions: Forget about offering answers, solutions, or free coaching. Tempting as it may be to offer a "sample coaching" session, resist the urge. It diminishes your status and pulls you away from your leadership position. Instead, wield the power of strategic questioning. Craft questions that serve four essential purposes:
   - *#1:* Vet them as the right clients for you (remember your ideal client's psychographics?)
   - *#2:* Help them gain clarity and depth about their own problems (people often downplay their challenges and bury their heads in the sand). Illuminate their pain because true transformation begins when they confront it head-on.
   - *#3:* As they understand what they want to replace their current problematic situation with, show them who they need to become in order to achieve the result they want instead of only focusing on the actions they need to take. Get them to see the difference between the current state

they are in and the future state of aspirational identity embodiment.

- *#4:* Demonstrate that you hold the solution to their problem and help them envision the possibilities ahead (remember, focus on the "what" but not the "how" so you don't end up free-coaching). But be cautious, avoid alleviating their pain during the call, as it provides instant relief, and they won't sign up with you! We both know that momentary relief isn't the same as true, lasting transformation that requires time and effort. Don't rob them of their discomfort; it's the fuel that ignites their desire for change.

3. Relate your methodology to their specific situation: If your marketing and offer positioning have been on point, dear Leader, the sales call is where you simply connect the dots. Avoid the rookie mistake of over-explaining the delivery details (the number of calls, videos, etc.). Your client doesn't care about that — unless they ask, of course! What they truly need to know is how your methodology will solve their problem. Focus on that.

4. Clarity and simplicity in your offer delivery and pricing: Be crystal clear about what you're selling and be prepared to answer questions without overcomplicating things. Decide in advance the price you will quote and stick to it. Don't waver or lower it during the call. Hold the value of your offer sacred. If you have a payment plan, have the numbers ready and written out so you don't have to figure them out in front of the client.

5. Embrace objections as part of the journey: Understand that objections are a natural part of human nature. Worry and doubt tend to arise, this is just human. But here's the truth: It's never about you — it's always about them. Their objections stem from limiting beliefs and karmic blocks. Your role is to stand strong as a leader who champions the Soul that brought them (the human) to you in the first place. Don't buy into their fears, my visionary friend. Hold space for

their transformation and the highest Vision (their aspirational identity) and guide them towards breaking free.

You've got this, badass Leader! Embrace the structure, infuse it with YOUR unique energy, and let your artistry shine through every sales call. Make sure you journal the hell out of this to create customized to your Soul Design sales structure so you are able to close these sales calls with a resounding "yes" without even trying!

Now you are ready to go out there and make sales-magic happen! And next we will look at that marketing message of yours that might need to be adjusted to generate these awesome sales calls.

Key Takeaways from Step 3 of The Conscious F.U.T.U.R.E. Method:

❖ **Ensuring that your sales calls are filled with the right prospects begins with your due diligence in creating a clear Methodology and Offer based on your Signature System. Sales success hinges on your unapologetic ability to clearly convey the value of what you do and why your prospects absolutely need it.** This mastery encompasses both the practical and linear aspects of knowing what to do and say, as well as the energetic and non-linear aspects of how to say it. Energetics hold immense power in magnetically attracting the perfect people who resonate with you and desire what you offer.

❖ To unlock your sales power, focus on three critical areas:

1. **Cleanse outdated beliefs and energy blockages** that hinder your ability to receive higher fees.

2. **Get your practical ducks in a row** by ensuring your Method incorporates your Soul Expertise, your Offer aligns with your authentic Soul Design Strategy, and your marketing effectively showcases your Method while consistently selling in your content.

3. **Master the art of conveying trustworthiness and expertise,** guiding clients with power, clarity, and love. Remember, it's not just about the words you speak; it's about the confident energy you exude. Subconsciously, your potential clients will feel the magnetic pull, irresistibly drawing them closer to you.

❖ **During your Soul-led sales calls, prioritize authentic connection and transformation of the Vision-based Sales process.** It's not about guilting, pressuring, or manipulating prospects into working with you. Instead, expand their perspective to see the real problem and position yourself as the solution by embodying the Identity they aspire to become. **To achieve high conversions, demonstrate leadership, ask strategic questions, relate your Methodology to their specific situation, be clear on your offer delivery and pricing, and as a leader, guide your prospects through objections** toward their own growth.

STEP 4: Upgrade Your Marketing Message

Dear Leader, I know you're a total badass coach with a unique gift for helping humanity level up their consciousness. Whether it's personal transformation, relationship, energetics, leadership, ancestral healing, goddess empowerment, body healing, self-love, life purpose — whatever you do, it's all in the "not-tangible" category of sales, right?

Let's talk stats. It's easier to sell a hard offer — something tangible that you can measure or calculate in practical terms. Think helping someone score a promotion by boosting their confidence or guiding them through a weight loss protocol you've developed. If you're good at what you do and you're selling a hard offer, you should be closing 4 out of 10 sales calls with ease, with a simple, clear system in place.

But what about soft offers — those intangible services that can't be easily measured or defined? If this is you, then consider yourself lucky because these are my specialty, and this book is for you! If you've got all your obvious ducks in a row, you should be closing about 1 out of every 15 sales calls with people you don't know — that's the market standard.

But wait, there's more! My methodology is all about utilizing your Soul Design in everything — from business strategy and offer delivery to messaging and lead generation. My clients who've adopted this approach typically have a close rate of 4-5 out of 10 — that's right, even higher than the market standard for hard offers! Living your Soul Design not only brings you happiness, but it also boosts your conversion rates and takes your business to the next level.

Let me tell you, I am so damn passionate about this topic, it's almost ridiculous. To me, the intangible offers are even more crucial than the tangible ones. Look, I get it, we all want a done-for-you service that will magically transform our lives, but let's be real here: true personal transformation, finding your purpose, becoming a leader — that comes from people like us. The ones who are tapping into multi-D and intuition, communicating with non-physical beings, and daring do our own personal inner work (which is not for the faint-hearted!). We are courageous enough to dream big and create real change in the world.

But here's the thing, *when you don't know how to articulate the value of your work to a prospective client and you can't get them to see the incredible impact your services can have on their life, it makes things a whole lot harder.* And I'm not just talking about a little bit harder, I'm talking about frustrating, crunchy, difficult clients who drain you of your energy and leave you wondering why the hell you ever got into this line of work in the first place.

Believe me, I've been there. I've had those clients who just don't seem to "get it" no matter how much heart and Soul I poured into their transformation. The ones who seem incapable of taking the steps needed to create the life they so desperately desire. And the worst part? This happens because we, the coaches, don't know how to communicate the value of our work effectively.

But now? Now, things are different. Because I've learned the power of having the perfect words to say to a prospective client, words that make them sit up and say, "Hell yes, sign me up!" Having the ability to clearly articulate the value of your work is the key to scaling your vision to multi-6 or 7-figures.

So trust me when I say this: if you're struggling to attract the right clients or getting too many wrong ones, if you're tired of dealing with difficult, uncommitted clients who drain your energy, then it's time to learn the art of aligned communication. It's time to master the art of selling your intangible offers with the same ease and effectiveness as a tangible offer. And I'm here to show you how.

First, we want to make sure we are clear on your *MMM — Meaningful Marketing Message.* This is the foundational piece of any marketing — you want to be able to explain what you do in a very short wording. Why is MMM important? Not only does it position you in the marketplace, but you can use it everywhere: In your Facebook and LinkedIn taglines, in your posts and videos, on your website, in your sales calls, and many more places.

Grab your journal for a moment and write out your MMM:

I help _________________ (who they are/niche) to _________________ (get specific result they want) without _________________ (what they don't want) by _________________ (your unique thing).

It doesn't have to follow this structure exactly but should have all the elements and be succinct.

Some examples for you:
- *I help women over 50 effortlessly shed 20 lbs without rigid diets or grueling gym sessions, utilizing the transformative power of the Zero-Point Hypnosis method.*
- *I help spiritual seekers liberate themselves from generational karma with a gentle reset of their DNA for profound healing, without getting caught up in over-processing.*
- *I guide powerful women into professional authentic leadership, without sacrificing their femininity, through my transformative Feminine Leadership method.*
- *I help spiritual coaches and healers create 6+ figure empires without endless hustle, pressure, or forcing, by leveraging their unique badass expertise and Soul Design Strategy. (MINE)*

Did you write yours out? You'll need it later for writing your converting message! ☺

Now that you've got your MMM, let me show you a deeply connecting and value-based way to speak to your ideal client — in your social media posts, in your emails, blogs, video content, sales pages in funnels, etc.

Below I'm sharing with you the **8-part anatomy framework** of a converting message that will make ANY post irresistible to your audience. *This framework can be used across all platforms, not only for short or long posts, or articles for a magazine or blog, but as a livestream or a video presentation structure — on Facebook, Instagram, LinkedIn, funnels, etc.*

This structure will ensure that your words resonate with the subconscious mind of your readers. And when you tap into the energetics of Quantum subconscious, people won't be able to resist reading your posts! Oh, and by the way, this structure works like magic for your sales page and marketing copy too!

🔥 HOOK: We start with a bang. This is where you grab your audience's attention and intrigue them. Make it interesting, even shocking! It could be a thought-provoking question or a glimpse of the problem you're about to solve. But whatever you do, don't give away the answer just yet! Many coaches make a rookie mistake of making this a "title" for their post — don't, trust me, it will sabotage its readability.

❤ EMPATHY: Now it's time to connect on an emotional level, my dear. Show your audience that you understand their struggles. Expand on the topic introduced in the hook or dive into something emotional that will resonate with their hearts. Let them know you expertly understand their situation, or that you've been there too, and that you care deeply. It's all about building that soulful connection. Use your intuition to summarize their feelings in bullets if you're confident, but make sure it flows seamlessly with the rest of your post.

✹ ASPIRATIONAL IDENTITY: Here's where you tap into the Higher Self of your readers. Speak to who they want to be seen as or who they secretly believe themselves to be. We want to break through those subconscious objections that say, "This is all just hype," or "It won't work for me." Lift them up and help them believe that change is possible, and possible specifically for them. Remind them of their dreams, the transformation they desire, and the positive emotional experiences they crave. This portion doesn't have to be lengthy. A single sentence, or a few lines of text, or visually appealing bullets will do the trick.

🖋 TOPIC itself: Now, let's get down to the nitty-gritty. If it's a Problem/Problem post, unravel the misconception and show them how they've been mistaking something on the surface for the real deeper issue. For Problem/Solution posts, reveal the solution they've been searching for. Problem/Gap posts call for defining the gap they need to bridge. And in Problem/Example posts, showcase your solution through a relatable example. Pick ONE of these (P/P, P/S, P/G or P/E) and stick to it. Keep this section visually appealing and engaging.

♛ EXPERTISE: This is where you want to mention your expertise directly to let the reader know you've got the knowledge and experience to back it up. This is the place for your MMM — Meaningful Marketing Message. One or two short sentences will suffice.

✸ BULLETS portion: Time to hit them with the goods! Present the answers they've been seeking in a "boom, boom, boom" format. Our brains love to save energy, so we want to make it easy for them to digest the information. It could be three solutions, five things not to do, or a list that resonates with their experiences. Get creative! Stay concise. The key is to provide clear and organized answers to the very reason they started reading your post.

🗯️ SUMMARY portion: Let's wrap it up, dear Leader! Summarize what you've just explained in a casual and relatable way. Keep it conversational. Remind them of the emotional state they were in and how following the steps or solutions you provided will lead them to their desired outcome. This can be a single longish sentence or a few lines but remember NOT to introduce any new information at this point! It's all about reinforcing the benefit and "what's in it for them."

🔔 CTA portion: Ah, the grand finale! Never underestimate the power of a well-crafted call-to-action, my dear. This is where you guide your readers on what to do next. Make it conversational, not official. Avoid generic phrases like "For more info, contact me." Instead, offer them options that engage and involve them. You could ask them to apply to work with you by directing them to a link in the comments or requesting them to leave a specific word in the comments. Alternatively, you can prompt them to answer a question or leave an emoji to gauge their interest. Get creative and make it irresistible!

There you have it, my dear! With this format, you'll effortlessly captivate your audience, ignite their curiosity, and guide them toward transformation. Keep in mind that this framework can be used across all messaging and media.

Here is an example post I wrote so you can see how it all comes together.

Are you tired, my fellow spiritual coach?

Exhausted by working with low-end peeps, feeling drained by random social media posts, frustrated with crunchy needy clients?

I understand the struggle, darling.

It hurts your Soul to pour your energy into clients who aren't the right fit.

You know you're undercharging and yet it feels so hard to find people who would pay premium, right?

This makes you question your worth despite the incredible results your clients are having.

And so you try even harder, only to feel that burnout might be around the corner. AGAIN!

Doubts start creeping in...

> *...what if your offer is not as good as you think?*

> *...what if nobody will pay high-ticket for your magic?*

> *...what if you're not caught out to become a millionaire after all?*

You are secretly embarrassed that you are not there yet...

With all the work you've put in, all the sacrifices you've made, all the transformation and healing you put yourself through, you should be there by now, damn it, right!?

But fear not, for you are not alone on this journey.

Close your eyes and envision your future. You are a high-end coach, serving clients who value your soulful expertise. Your million-dollar empire is within reach, and you radiate confidence in your divine purpose. How does that feel?

Here's the revelation, my love.

The biggest misconception here is that you simply "need more high-end clients".

That somehow if you found a location where these high-ticket peeps congregate, you will be able to show up, say what you are now saying, and they will whip out their credit cards.

That "more clients" will solve all the problems…

This is simply not true. If it was, everyone would just be running ads to mediocre sales pages and becoming millionaires.

You and I both know there is more to it than that!

Allow me to introduce myself. I am Eugenia Oganova, a business strategist and messaging energetics coach with over 20 years of experience. I've helped countless clients save years of pressure and forcing themselves into ineffective strategies, guiding them towards their Soul Design Strategy and remarkable results.

Let me ask you a question:

If you ask your clients, what did you do for them, will they all be able to answer clearly? Will they all say the same thing?

Or will they offer stuff like "oh, so many things" and "it's beyond words amazing"?

So believe me when I tell you that the issue here is not lack of some unicorn perfect clients who never utter an objection and always pay in full, but …

… lack of clarity in your own message!

What you truly need are these 3 things:

1. *Uncover your Soul Design, the essence of energetics and strategy for your mission, tap into that unique blueprint to ignite a profound sense of fulfillment. This will give you clarity on your larger vision, so you embody the correct frequency.*

2. *Get clear on who these ideal peeps are who would deeply appreciate your premium services, align with your mission, and able to afford you. This way you can spy on their every breath and learn all their desires, fears, issues, and construct truly converting content for them.*

3. *Learn to articulate the immense value of your soul's superpower within your offers, enabling you to communicate with clarity and confidence, captivating your audience and inspiring them to embrace the transformative power of your gifts.*

So, my dear coach, by embracing your Soul Design Strategy and skillfully communicating the value of your superpower, you will effortlessly attract the perfect clients. Say goodbye to burnout and hello to fulfilling and abundant relationships with those who truly appreciate your divine gifts.

Are you ready to transform your coaching business and manifest the success you desire?

Let's embark on this journey together.

Book a call with me, and we'll delve into what's currently happening in your business. I'll provide you with valuable advice and show you how my expertise can guide you to extraordinary heights.

The first step is just a click away! Aren't you tired of going it alone?

Leave your favorite emoji below and I will message you to set up the call. Can't wait to meet you!

I want you to actually create a post using my Conscious F.U.T.U.R.E. 8-part anatomy framework. Get your laptop and write it out. This is what you need for a converting post.

Please don't just change a few words and copy my sample post above, your ideal clients are waiting to hear YOUR style and voice from you, not mine!

To write your own converting post, start by deciding on what the Message is.

What do you want to say?

Which problem does it solve for your ideal client?

Why do they need to read it?

What do they desire?

How can you help?

Which format do you want to focus on: (P/P, P/S, P/G or P/E)

What is your writing style? (TIP: it is linked to your Archetypes!)

Your ability to communicate the value of your work through compelling content is key. With powerful messaging, you will never have to worry about whether your ideal clients understand what you do. Instead, they will be raising their hands, wanting to work with you. In fact, if you do this right, they may even sell themselves to you on the sales calls ☺

You've got this, love! 🖤

Key Takeaways from Step 4 of The Conscious F.U.T.U.R.E. Method:

❖ Mastering the art of communicating the value of your work through captivating content is paramount. **Without the ability to articulate this value to prospective clients, selling your offer becomes challenging,** attracting difficult clients who drain your energy and leave you questioning what you're saying to attract them in the first place.

❖ A Meaningful Marketing Message forms the foundation of any successful marketing endeavor. **It is crucial to be able to clearly explain what you do in a concise manner.** Utilize this message in your Facebook and LinkedIn taglines, posts, videos, website, presentations, and sales calls to create a consistent and impactful presence.

> ❖ **Leverage my 8-part anatomy framework for a converting message and watch as your posts become irresistible to your audience across all platforms.** This framework can be applied to short or long posts, magazine articles, blog entries, live streams, video presentations, and funnels. **By resonating with the subconscious mind of your readers through this structure, you tap into the powerful energetics of the Quantum subconscious,** leaving people unable to resist reading your posts.
>
> ❖ With a powerful messaging strategy in place, you can release any concerns about whether your ideal clients truly understand what you offer. Instead, they will eagerly raise their hands, expressing a desire to work with you. In fact, **when executed correctly, your ideal clients may even sell themselves to you during sales calls,** recognizing the undeniable value you bring to their lives.

STEP 5: Ramp Up Your Lead Generation Strategy

Lead Generation is the lifeblood of your business. It's time to build your authority and attract high-paying clients by choosing the right marketing efforts. In doing so, consistency and sustainability are key. It's important to find the right lead generation for your unique Soul Design so that you can maintain your efforts and avoid burnout.

In the past, we had limited options for reaching our audience — we had to buy TV commercial time, place ads in newspapers, or if you were a bootstrapping type, pin hand-made flyers on a bulletin board in a local yoga studios or health food stores. And even then, the reach was often small and localized, unless you had a lot of money to spend.

But that's all changed now. With social media, you have access to the entire global market. And it's not just a nice-to-have anymore — if you want to find and attract your ideal clients, you need to expand your reach to the entire globe. Social media is the way to connect with your audience, educate them about your unique approach, and invite them into your world.

If you're hesitant about social media, take a look at the subconscious judgments and visibility fears that may be holding you back. Nothing is inherently good or bad — it's all neutral, and it's up to us to know how to use it. But I see so many coaches being super busy with all sorts of marketing activities online, only to be stressed, frustrated, and still not manifesting the desired results.

Unfortunately, many marketing programs out there teach you that you have to do all the marketing activities all the time to bring clients in. In my world of Conscious F.U.T.U.R.E. Method we replace "getting leads" with "attracting potential clients."

Why? There is a reason you are having an emotional allergic reaction to "getting leads" — it is based in scarcity. The mindset here is: you "don't have leads", you need to "go get leads". As we know, *the Universe doesn't speak English, it speaks Frequency*, so if you are broadcasting scarcity, you won't get abundance — you will get more scarcity.

Running around frantically trying to implement every trending tactic doesn't do anything good for your sanity or your lead generation. It only creates drama and pressure, leading straight into burnout.

Or are you the type who wants to do everything right, who's invested a ton of cash in courses about how to hack the Facebook algorithm or get views on YouTube or create complex funnels with five different software tools? And you spend months tweaking and perfecting your setup, only to hit "go" and hear crickets chirping? Oh honey, that's going to leave you feeling bitter, and even worse, it might make you start doubting your Mission and give up altogether.

And what about you, the emotional rebel who thinks *"I shouldn't have to post on social media all the time, I just need to vibrate at a higher frequency and the Universe will send me clients"?* Well, good luck with that! If you don't show up and create some serious visibility for yourself, you'll be stuck with just your current circle of influence, and we all know that word-of-mouth isn't a reliable business strategy.

So let's deal with the real issue here: your fear of failure, your fear of success, your fear of being judged or not knowing what to say or do on social media. It's time to stop making excuses and start showing up like the true Leader you are!

Yes, vibrating at a higher frequency that aligns with your Soul is an absolute game-changer for your *Wealth Energetics* (and more on this is coming in Chapters 8 and 9). But let me tell you something — frequency itself is not a strategy. It's more like an upgrade to the strategy you already got going on. Like if you're already crushing it with your marketing, and showing up every damn day, then adding in that sweet, multi-D vibration is like adding fuel to a fire. It's going to make that flame burn brighter and hotter than ever before. This is the Quantum Creation stuff.

But here's the thing, my dear Leader. Your Soul, your energy guides, God-Source — they can only give you a hand and point you in the right direction if you're already moving. If you're standing still, stuck in perfectionism paralysis or just plain avoiding your lead generation, then they can't do anything for you.

You've always got to take that first step, Soul Sister. And once you do, you'll see — the Universe is going to have your back in ways you couldn't have even dreamed of.

If you remember, at the beginning of this book we talked about your Soul Design Strategy. Yes, the one that sets you apart from the rest of the world, the one that's unique to YOU. And guess what, that applies to your lead generation too.

I'm not talking about doing all the latest tactics or posting 10 times a day like a robot and essentially polluting already clogged social space with more junk that no one needs or wants.

No, no, no. That's not how we, conscious badass Leaders, operate, now is it?

Correct lead generation is all about YOU.

It's tailored to your unique energetics, and when it's done right, it feels like second nature. You don't even have to think about it!

But first, let's make sure you understand the foundations you must have in place for successful Soul-aligned client attraction:
* You have to know your expertise and know who it is for (we covered this in Chapter 7, step 1).
* Have a clear methodology that your signature offer is based on (this is in Chapter 7, Step 2).
* Able to sell your offer in your content and over the sales calls with confidence (Chapter 7, Step 3).
* Intimately understand your ideal client and be able to articulate the value of your work in converting ways (this is covered in Chapter 7, Step 4).

Now, with all that in place, setting up a specific lead generation strategy is a breeze!

Have you just had a massive realization?

You see, all that time and energy you've been putting into posting on social media (or even spending money on ads) was for naught because you didn't have the foundational pieces in place? Or some were missing and required fine-tuning?

But no worries, this is a skill you can learn, and once you do, the socials will be begging for a piece of you! You can leverage your priceless individuality by combining solid linear strategies with nonlinear Quantum Creation and Wealth Energetics. This will allow you to collapse time and add nonlinear magic to your consistent efforts, skyrocketing your results. In Chapters 8 and 9 I will tell you more about the non-linear stuff, here we will focus on the linear parts.

Ready to uncover your ideal lead generation strategy, aligned with your Soul Design and Archetypes? It's time to tap into your intuition and trust that the perfect approach will flow effortlessly for you. Let's dive into these 14 questions, designed to guide you towards the most natural and authentic way to attract your ideal clients. This will blow your mind and give you so much relief!

Remember, Leader, this should feel like a soulful dance, not like pulling teeth! Any preconceived notions or limiting beliefs may try to block your path to implementing a strategy. So, it's crucial to shift yourself into a state of neutrality, release those emotional reactions, and instead, attune your Soul and Body to the whispers of divine guidance.

It's almost time for another journaling session — it's coming up!

Dear magical badass Leader, I want to take a moment to honor and appreciate the effort and time you're investing in completing these exercises. Let me assure you that this upfront work will pave the path for your business to soar to magnificent heights of multi-6 or 7-figures. And here's the beauty of it all — you won't have to struggle, pressure yourself, or chase after fleeting trends that zoom by your social media feed.

In **Conscious F.U.T.U.R.E. Mastery** I put my clients through almost 20 questions to fine-tune their lead generation. Here, so as not to overwhelm you, we will look at the top 5 to help you get the taste (and clarity!) Believe me, understanding how your Soul Design aligns with your lead generation strategy will be the catalyst that propels you towards the RESULTS your heart craves. I have unwavering faith in your abilities. You've got this!

Get your journal, and let's do this.

1. Are you a natural networker? Does the art of connecting with people make your heart sing? *(Especially resonant for the Nurturer, Romantic, and Innocent archetypes)*

If YES, then embrace the power of Facebook group posting strategy (when you share your posts into many relevant Facebook groups 3 times per week), engaging in Messenger conversations, fostering deep communication with those who comment on your posts. You don't need to create endless freebies, instead post small conversational bites and expand your network by befriending kindred spirits on Facebook, Instagram, and LinkedIn. Keep mentioning your expertise though, so they know you can help them more if they work with you! You can also attend in-person networking events or create a Meetup in your area.

If NO, don't fret about Messenger, cold "connection calls", or drowning in endless comments. These draining activities are not aligned with your energy and vitality.

2. Do you have an inherent love for teaching and enjoy the delight of being asked questions, my wise one? (Especially resonant for the Ruler, Alchemist, and Sage)

If YES, let your brilliance shine through engaging livestreams on Facebook or Instagram, or deliver captivating presentations to audiences in Facebook groups, summits, or in-person events and conferences. Share your wisdom and ignite the minds of those who seek your guidance. You also might want to create high-value free gifts that you promote on your social networks and email, and as people join your list, share more with them about working with you.

3. Are you a master wordsmith, Soul Sister, reveling in crafting tantalizing sentences that stir desire?

If YES, then let your words dance upon the page! Create daily written content that entices and compels, luring your audience with irresistible calls to action that lead them to work with you. You might want to simplify by creating one piece of content per day, then posting it on all social media accounts and sending it as an email to your list. This builds intimate connections and, if you keep gracefully selling in your writing, they will come.

4. Does the idea of constant creation feel overwhelming, my focused friend? Would you rather masterfully complete one thing and then have it in place, allowing you to repeat and refine it?

If YES, my dear, you have two exquisite options to consider. Firstly, immerse yourself in live webinars, where you can harness the power of repetition to refine and perfect your message. Conduct a live online training that serves as the cornerstone of your lead generation strategy, a webinar that you lovingly fine-tune and continuously improve. This is your opportunity to gather market proof, as you engage with your audience in real-time and witness the resonance of your presentation and offer. During these live webinars, your aim is not only to educate and inspire but to guide your attendees towards signing up for your offer, right then and there. Allow your webinar topic to be purposeful and intentional, ensuring that it impeccably aligns with the key components of your unique methodology. Unveil the step-by-step process of your signature system, empowering your audience with transformative insights.

Remember, *refinement is the secret ingredient to success*. Just as I honed my 30-minute webinar presentation through 16 live deliveries to discover the winning combination, even Russell Brunson of ClickFunnels presented his webinar in-person a staggering 100 times before transitioning it into an evergreen masterpiece. The essence is to ensure that your webinar not only addresses objections but effortlessly compels your potential clients to take action, bringing them one step closer to embracing your offer. Once you have gotten the winning structure and witnessed its irresistibility firsthand, it's time to transform your live webinar into an evergreen asset. It will guide prospects towards a sales call with you, where you can further nurture their journey and present the depth of your transformative offer. As you solidify this refined approach, consider going on podcasts and promoting it, or amplifying your reach by adding strategic paid advertising to your evergreen webinar, allowing more souls to be drawn into your funnel.

Alternatively, if you possess a knack for writing, leverage your talent to create high-level professional, compelling, converting content. Once perfected, schedule your pre-written posts to be shared daily on social media and posted on your blog as well, automating your presence while maintaining a consistent flow of engaging material. Bear in mind, to ensure their conversion power, test these posts on social media first and refine them until they become high-converting gems and you get lots of comments and responses. Over time, you'll build a vast library of these potent converting posts (I myself have over 300), and you'll only need to create new ones whenever inspiration strikes.

5. Are you the laid-back behind-the-scenes girl? You feel the best when you just invite people into your life and share the moment?

If YES, this is your time to shine as the nonchalant leader, effortlessly inviting people into your life and sharing captivating moments. Embrace the power of your cell phone camera and unleash your creativity through spontaneous recordings. Whenever you feel that delightful spark of inspiration, that inner knowing that what you have to share can profoundly impact your clients, seize the moment without hesitation. There's no need to wait until you're home in front of your computer. Instead, grab your camera and dive into the world of live streaming on Facebook or Instagram (Instagram stories and reels work wonders here). Embrace the raw and authentic nature of these videos, allowing your true essence to shine through. Remember, in these moments, you must infuse your expertise seamlessly and naturally, guiding your viewers towards a clear and compelling call to action. Weave your CTA into the fabric of your video, making it abundantly clear why they should reach out to you on DMs immediately to set up a call. Let the magic of your candid recordings become a portal through which your ideal clients can effortlessly connect with you, igniting their desire to purchase.

***

Alright, let's talk about an example of how Soul Design can be aligned with the lead generation, and other components of business we've looked into so far — we'll call her Mary.

She's a beautiful soul with a slow and steady flow. She's the type of person who, once she knows what to do, could keep doing it forever and grow her business into the millions. But here's the thing — Mary was feeling lost and directionless. She spent countless hours researching new techniques, getting certifications, and creating programs that she could only sell for $1500. She was barely breaking even, and constantly pouring her hard-earned profits into the next certification, the next freelancer, the next sales funnel. It was soul-killing, exhausting, and not sustainable. She tried to be spontaneous in her videos and just felt embarrassed, tried to chat on messenger and felt out of integrity. All of the strategies she saw others do felt too flashy and glamorous, and she felt forced as she pressured herself to show up.

But here's the good news: Mary's Soul Design is that of a workhorse. She can take on a lot and pay incredible attention to details — but to what end? Together, we created one signature offer that brought together all of her skills and expertise. We dialed in her message, priced it at $15k, and streamlined everything from onboarding to delivery. And the best part? We created a series of free 5-day meticulously crafted events, with workbooks and emails, that she could deliver with ease of her expertise. Now, Mary doesn't have to keep searching, go live from her car, or chat on messenger — she can focus on selling on these events four times per year, and on increasing client retention. She can hire a team and a support coach, fine-tune her automations, and generate more income while working less. Mary is set to scale to a million, all while staying true to her beautiful, steady flow.

***

Let me give you an example of a client who had the opposite Soul Design and lead generation from Mary. Let's call her Dinarah. Dinarah's Soul Design was that of a creative igniter. She had the potential to spark a massive fire of productivity and inspiration, but she lacked consistency. Dinarah was struggling with sporadic income because she would go from one program to the next without any structure or strategy. One month she would be excited and sell a program without any plan by going live everywhere, the next month she would dread doing anything at all. Believing her problem was lack of structure, she forced herself to create email sequences, write posts following someone's template, and create webinars. She would over-give to the point of exhaustion, and she would have periods where no clients would come because she didn't feel inspired to market anything.

To solve this, we first worked on elevating her frequency. Instead of constantly hopping from offer to offer, we looked at the larger theme and linked her Soul Expertise to it. Then, we created one offer that could be scaled. We found the best lead generation strategy that matched her Soul Design — monthly free webinars. These could be done with minimal prep and promo, but Dinarah simply chatting excitedly about each new adventure she cooked up for her peeps. This allowed her to do something new every time she felt inspired, but because we picked one thing that fit Dinarah, all of these events funneled prospects into her offer. We simplified the delivery of the offer by recording most of it on videos once, so Dinarah could simply show up and coach. This way, she could scale her business and create a sustainable situation for herself.

***

By now you should have gained some clarity on which lead generating strategies align beautifully with your unique Soul Design and Archetypes. Armed with this knowledge, it's time to take decisive action. Whether it involves creating a well-defined procedure and diligently following it, crafting compelling content and scheduling it for maximum impact, organizing and promoting a free challenge, or engaging with other influential leaders to set up a summit, it's crucial to *implement* the chosen strategy effectively.

I understand that this process can feel overwhelming at times, but fear not, for you are not alone. As part of my mission to empower and support my clients, my team and I are here to assist you in getting your lead generation strategy in order (among other things☺). We can guide you through the creation of an engaging free conversion event, complete with expertly crafted emails and opt-in pages. We can help you host an impactful summit, taking care of guest acquisition, page setup, and email management. Furthermore, we can collaborate on crafting and refining your workshops and webinars, ensuring they become evergreen assets that consistently generate leads. (And our VIP containers can even help you create all these automated funnels on the backend to guide leads through the buying process while you sleep!)

Keep in mind, my dear Leader, you don't have to navigate this journey by yourself. If you're getting great results with your clients and seeking assistance in optimizing your lead generation to unleash your full potential, don't hesitate to reach out to us: eugeniaoganova.com/start

Key Takeaways from Step 5 of
The Conscious F.U.T.U.R.E. Method:

❖ **Lead Generation is the lifeblood of your business, but it's essential to find a style that aligns with your unique Soul Design, allowing you to sustain your efforts without hardship or burnout.** By combining solid linear strategies with nonlinear Quantum Creation and Wealth Energetics, you can leverage your priceless individuality, collapsing time and leading to exponential results.

❖ **In the Conscious F.U.T.U.R.E. Method, we replace the notion of "getting leads" with "attracting potential clients"** because the former is rooted in scarcity. When you operate from a mindset of "not having leads" and needing to "go get leads," you broadcast scarcity to the Universe, attracting more of the same. Since the Universe communicates through frequency, **it's crucial to radiate abundance in order to receive abundance.**

❖ Frantically chasing after every trending tactic does not contribute positively to your sanity or lead generation. It only creates drama and pressure, inevitably leading to burnout. Likewise, obsessively attempting to crack social media algorithms, or spending months on end with no responses, will leave you feeling bitter and questioning your mission. Believing that you don't need to actively engage on social media and that clients will come to you through vibrational alignment only is a flawed approach. **Without creating visibility and actively showing up, you will be limited to your current circle of influence, and relying on word-of-mouth is NOT a business strategy.**

- ❖ Addressing the underlying issues related to fear of failure, fear of success, fear of judgment, and uncertainty about what to say or do on social media is the key to sustainable lead generation. It's crucial to overcome your own obstacles, stop making excuses, and step into the role of a true leader. **Your Soul, energy guides, and the Divine Source can only support and guide you if you are already taking action.** Standing still in perfectionism paralysis or avoiding lead generation will hinder their ability to assist you.
- ❖ **Foundational elements for successful Soul-aligned client attraction** include:
  - Knowing your expertise and identifying your target audience.
  - Having a clear methodology that forms the foundation of your signature offer.
  - Effectively selling your offer with confidence in your content and sales calls.
  - Developing an intimate understanding of your ideal client and effectively articulating the value of your work in a compelling and converting manner.
- ❖ **Clarifying which lead generation strategies beautifully align with your unique Soul Design and Archetypes is paramount.** This may involve establishing a well-defined procedure and diligently following it, crafting compelling content and strategically scheduling it for maximum impact, organizing and promoting a free challenge, or collaborating with influential leaders to set up a summit. **The key is *implementing* your chosen strategy effectively to attract and engage your ideal clients.**

STEP 6: Elevate & Scale Your Business

Scaling is the next frontier, and we achieve it by tapping into the power of automation and assembling a dream team, balanced by streamlined delivery and nurturing your clients. In this Step we will look at these *3 most essential components that simplify scaling of your business:*
* Automation and Team,
* Onboarding and Delivery Support,
* Nurture.

Ready?

Here you are, standing on the edge of taking your business to the next level — scaling it up. It's an exciting time, but it can also be overwhelming. That's why it's important to *streamline your operations and delivery to elevate your business as a whole, have support, and plug all the leaks.*

I've seen it all, and let me tell you, when my clients first come to me, they're often stuck in some version of what they think is a business strategy, but often it's nothing more than some kind of clunky, bootlegged version of success that's only going to leave you feeling burnt out, broke, and batshit crazy. Trust me, dear, it's time to ditch the struggle and start living the life and business you were born for!

* If you're still stuck on selling one-off low-end sessions as your main business model, then you're stuck trading time for money. And let me tell you, you're customizing for every client and letting them lead instead of leading, and that's a recipe for disaster! I mean, just look at the math: $100k per year = $8,300 per month = 83 sessions at $100 per month = about 20-40 hours per week (if you take no breaks to eat or

rest). That's no way to live your life! You'll be a slave to your business, and there's no room for you or your loved ones.

❖ Now, let's say you're selling mid-level offers, and you're able to sell a $1500 program 5 times per month. Well, that's better, but you're still running yourself ragged with marketing and sales calls. You're still going to have to hustle hard to sell that program 5 times every month just to hit 6-figures. This becomes too hard very quickly, and so you're launching a new offer every month, working 24-7, and always balancing between inspired and burnt out. All this effort to sell a $1500 program! And there's no way to scale this.

❖ Perhaps you're the type of healer who colors outside the lines and plays by your own rules. You've got this amazing $5k program that's practically oozing with magic, and all you need to do is sell 3 of them every two months to hit that coveted $100k mark. But you've got no clear strategy, you create a whole new program every few months, which means starting from scratch with your marketing, messaging, sales pages, opt-ins, and materials, a brand new funnel again — because when you communed with your guides on Tuesday, you got excited about yet another new direction (or because consistent methodology hasn't occurred to you!) This business model is practically impossible to scale!

❖ If you've got a signature higher ticket offer, priced at $10k, and you're clear on your value, message and methodology, then you're onto something. Because at this point, you only need to sell one program a month to hit $100k. That's less than 10 hours a week, leaving you plenty of time to market, innovate, and grow your business. And once you've got all the kinks worked out, then you can start thinking about scaling this baby up to 7-figures!

I hear you — maybe you're thinking, "I don't mind creating new marketing every time, I just can't stand doing the same thing over and over again!" Or perhaps you're saying, "I wish I could just set it up correctly once, but I have no clue what will actually work!" Here's the thing: there are as many unique Soul Designs as there are stars in the sky, over 2.5 million! Which means that, in reality, each of us is a one-of-a-kind masterpiece. So, when it comes to creating Wealth by your Soul Design, there's no one-size-fits-all strategy that's going to work for everyone.

What might feel wrong to you is not the strategy itself, but rather how it's being applied to you and your business.

But don't worry, my dear — in Chapters 8 and 9 I'll share more about *how to leverage the non-linear creation and personal mastery to help you further.* For now, let's identify any holes or energy leaks that are holding you back and plug them up so you can scale.

Automations and Team

In Step #5, we dove into Lead Generation strategies and now it's time to experiment with strategies that create pure magic by tapping into the power of automation and assembling a dream team. We're talking about finding that winning combo of a few strategies that feel natural for you to implement, and you know what to do and say so that it converts the best.

Beware, my friend, for I've witnessed the greatest sabotage of all. As coaches hit six figures, they sprint to hire everyone under the sun. There's a dangerous notion circulating that "embracing the goddess energy" and "manifesting ease and flow" demands a massive entourage. Now, I adore the concept of hiring before you feel entirely ready, but I'm not on board with hiring for the sake of it, falling prey to an image of success that involves being pampered and waited on while leaking profits.

Never outsource from a place of fear or insecurity.

So, who do you truly need when you're crossing that glorious six-figure threshold and beyond? Enter *the assistant*, your right-hand aficionado of daily maintenance, of support emails, of video transcribing and editing who slices your lengthy epics into tantalizing highlights. They'll seamlessly navigate the social media scheduler, and when your posts go live, they'll monitor the pulse of the audience, swift to respond. Depending on your strategy, they might even become a social media manager, the ambassador who reaches out, chats on your behalf, or orchestrates the scheduling of blog posts, social media updates, and emails.

Now, if you find yourself yearning for specific professional done-for-you solution, like tech wizardry to construct your funnels in the most converting way and teach you what stats to track, set up opt-in pages, program email sequences, or organize the backend of your operation — my team and I can help with that too. Our VIP containers, available to Conscious F.U.T.U.R.E. Mastery clients, can help you consolidate all your duct-taped software into one streamlined system, create automations using your magic words and methodology, and show you how you can simplify your tech once and for all without compromising quality.

Simply reach out at eugeniaoganova.com/start .

FYI: you only want to work with tech agencies that care to understand what you do and help you get better at saying it, instead of just using cookie-cutter templates. This is why I and my team support you in the alchemy of wording your magic first. Once you have gotten clear on your words and copy — then you can hire us to stick it into the right tech solutions to simplify your life!

Should you hire a copywriter?

Hear me loud and clear: Content creation and Sales are your divine domains for optimal conversions. You do NOT want to outsource them! Those aspects deserve your personal touch, for you are the sorceress of mesmerizing words and sales enchantment!

Now, envision a world where multiple launches unfurl one after another, automated email sequences dance in tune, video productions and social media events light up the stage. That's when you need an Online Business Manager (OBM). Unlike a mere Virtual Assistant, the OBM guides the teams and orchestrates intricate projects. They have the freedom to make decisions that shape your business, liberating you to your zone of genius.

How to hire the right people?

I can write a separate book on this, but here I will share with you 3 things I find are the most important for my type of client — and thus for you as well.

1. **Clarity on Action:** Get crystal clear on what you are looking for this person to do — none of this "they should just read my mind" stuff! Clearly define the tasks and responsibilities you seek to entrust to them. Leave no room for ambiguity or guesswork, although it's a process. Create standard operating procedures (SOPs) that your hire can open and follow through on with ease.
2. **The Dance of Psychographics:** Do you want them to be detail-oriented or visionary for the task? Do you need them to have a good creative eye or be amazing at just following directions without improvising? Specify the skills, qualifications, and experience required for the actions you want from them, ensuring that they can do it.
3. **Boundaries that Liberate:** What are the parameters here so you both know what to expect? This includes hours,

structure and frequency of communication, reporting, and your expectations.

Remember that the quest for the right people requires patience and discernment. Seek individuals whose values align with your own, for it is within this alignment that the true magic of collaboration emerges. In most situations, it is easier and more cost-effective to hire someone you can train but expect 3 to 6 months of learning period. If you want to hire professionals, expect to pay premium for high-level services. All of this still hinges on knowing your audience, your message and methodology, and embodying the frequency that your niche craves.

To summarize:
- ❖ Hire who you anticipate you will need based on your Soul Design Strategy and current business structure.
- ❖ Hire selectively, guided by wisdom rather than illusions.
- ❖ Hire to train if you want an assistant that does what you do.
- ❖ Hire professionals if you want them to do something better than you do now.

Let your coaching empire rise, radiating the essence of your genius, with all the support you need. Remember, scaling is an art, a dance with limitless possibilities. It requires not only structural expansion but also personal and energetic one.

Onboarding and Delivery support

What happens once a client signs up with you? Do you have a system in place to ensure their success? *It's crucial to have a well-structured support system ready to assist them right from the start.* There's nothing more frustrating than receiving an email from a client expressing second thoughts about their purchase, causing your heart to sink. To avoid this, it's essential to provide a clear pathway to support them.

For instance, consider implementing an automated welcome email sequence that acquaints them with the resources available to them. This could include setting up their password, accessing course materials, providing links to join your private Facebook group, or offering ways to connect via Voxer. You might consider sending them an automated voice recording or a personalized mini-video, adding a personal touch to their onboarding experience. As your business grows and you begin running group programs, it becomes essential to have pre-recorded video content that guides clients on how to achieve the best results while working with you. These videos can explain what is expected of them, how you communicate, the mindset they should adopt, and other relevant information.

Do you know when your clients typically start to experience doubts or struggle within your program? Yeap, it's natural, and you'll do much better if you anticipate it and handle it. It's often around the 35% mark, occasionally halfway through. It's crucial to have specific content available at that point to help them navigate this challenging phase. By providing targeted resources that address their concerns, you can ensure they don't feel left on their own or overwhelmed. Automating the delivery of this content allows you to offer support without needing to handle it personally or panicking when such situations arise. By acknowledging their potential feelings and automating the delivery of appropriate resources, you demonstrate that you understand their experience and are there to guide them.

Even in private offers, as you accumulate experience with numerous clients, you'll start recognizing the key elements they need to know at each step. Instead of spending valuable coaching call time on teaching these basics, I teach my clients to record instructional videos or audio materials that their clients can review beforehand. This approach maximizes the effectiveness of your coaching calls, focusing on what truly matters and yielding superior results.

Furthermore, incorporating checkpoints to assess your clients' progress is vital. Not only does this benefit you, but it also empowers your clients by showcasing how far they have come. Implementing check-ins at the end of each step of your program or at specific intervals (e.g., start, middle, and end) allows you to address their progress directly. This can be done through a designated part of the coaching call or by scheduling automated emails to be sent at the appropriate intervals.

As you transition to running group programs, you may require additional support to deliver them effectively. This entails leveraging automations, utilizing pre-recorded content, and structuring coaching calls to ensure that everyone's needs are met.

At this point, hiring a support coach or two can be immensely beneficial. Your program graduates often make excellent support coaches since they have firsthand experience with your offer and possess intimate knowledge of its intricacies. There are typically two types of support coaches:

1. **Motivation, Emotional Processing, and Mindset Coach:** This individual ensures that clients stay on track with your program, providing motivation, assisting with emotional processing, and helping them maintain the right mindset to avoid getting sidetracked.
2. **Specialist Coach:** These coaches possess specific skills outside your area of expertise. For example, if you're a weight loss and empowerment coach, a support coach with expertise in hypnosis could complement your services. Similarly, if you're a relationship coach, an energy healer

could serve as a valuable support coach. This way, you can provide comprehensive support to your clients by tapping into the strengths of others.

By carefully structuring your client support system and integrating automation, pre-recorded content, and support coaches, you can ensure a seamless and fulfilling experience for your clients while also allowing your business to scale and meet the growing demands of group programs. This strategic approach ensures that you can deliver high-quality support, address diverse needs, and optimize your clients' overall experience for ultimate magic!

Remember, building a successful program involves continuously refining and enhancing your support system. Regularly gather feedback from clients and assess the effectiveness of your resources, automations, and coaching processes. By staying attuned to their needs and making necessary adjustments, you can ensure that your clients feel fully supported throughout their journey with you, no matter how large your group program is.

Want to know how to guarantee amazing clients results?
- ❖ Get crystal clear on the epic journey you want your clients to experience, and hold your leadership position with unwavering focus, even when their doubts try to throw them (and you!) off course.
- ❖ Embody the role of a transformative teacher who instills self-responsibility and relentless follow-through in your clients, so they stay committed to their growth.
- ❖ Create a seamless structure of automated onboarding emails, personalized welcome messages, and captivating instructional resources that speak directly to their doubts and challenges.

❖ Design strategic progress checkpoints that you, or your superstar team, can effortlessly manage, ensuring no one gets left behind, especially when you're rocking it with larger groups.

❖ Remember, you don't have to carry the weight of it all — enlist the support of brilliant coaches who can handle the aspects that fall outside your zone of genius.

In summary, once someone signs up with you, it's crucial to remain a leader and empower commitment in your clients, have a logical clear structure in place, consistently check on the client's progress, and have support for yourself. By implementing these elements, you can ensure your clients' results and create an exceptional empowering experience that fosters long-term satisfaction.

And in the next segment, we will investigate nurturing of your potential and existing clients to ease lead generation and extend the lifecycle of each client to help you scale faster.

Nurture

Ah, the art of audience nurturing. *It's a delicate dance, finding the sweet spot between attracting new prospects and honoring those who have already invested in working with you.*

You see, there are two common extremes that can throw you off balance and block your ability to scale. On one end, you might be consumed with acquiring more and more new leads, neglecting those who may not have taken the leap just yet. On the other end, you might find yourself in a perpetual cycle of creating new offers to keep your loyal tribe entertained without truly evolving. It's time to unravel this paradox and create a harmonious path for scaling.

Your audience starts as cold leads, unaware of your existence but intrigued by the whispers of your message. As they warm up, they begin to trust you, yearning for what you offer, evolving into those coveted hot leads who seek the solution by purchasing your offer.

Cold leads are interested in your free social media content and compelling presentations, whether delivered virtually or in person. These serve as the portal through which they step into your world, mesmerized by the essence of your offerings and the promise of a solution to their problems.

The nurturing of warm leads is kindling the flames of trust, guiding them towards becoming sizzling hot leads who eagerly jump on your sales call, ready to sign up with you.

One of the most common mistakes I see coaches make is that they ignore this nurturing all together, just keep trying to get more and more people onto their lists, into their Facebook groups, more likes, more followers… And if the person didn't click, they are ignored as the coach moves onto the next potential lead. This is so wasteful and makes you work a million times harder!

Instead, *if you choose to keep the conversation going with the people who already entered your world, you have ease.* Engage them in meaningful dialogue, be it through messages, emails, or heartfelt replies. And when you create SOPs (Standard Operating Procedures) for these exchanges, you grant yourself the gift of ease. Empower your virtual assistant to take care of these nurturing conversations, freeing you to focus on the higher-level actions.

Embrace the power of automation, for it shall amplify your efforts and set you free. Segment your list, creating distinct email sequences tailored to those who have engaged with specific freebies or attended events. You can choose to lead them to purchase a VIP Day or a low-end mini course, before inviting them to your sales call to talk about working with you. Within the dance of nurture, follow up conversations, and automation, lies the key to scaling with grace, impact, and ease.

To summarize:
- ❖ Invite new people onto your list daily (aim for at least 10 qualified leads per day when you're starting).
- ❖ Create solid Standard Operating Procedures (SOPs) to guide these newcomers along a clear path, leading them from a free gift or video training to a small paid product to a sales call (or directly to that call if possible).
- ❖ Create or re-purpose content, tailored to attract and engage prospects at every stage of their exploration within your world.
- ❖ Automate most of it so you seal the leaks and don't lose people who need more time to become acquainted with you and your solution to their problem.

By harnessing the power of automation and team, streamlining your delivery processes, and nurturing your clients, you'll have all the tools you need to systemically scale. You've got this!

Congratulations, my dear! You've journeyed through my Conscious F.U.T.U.R.E. Method, unlocking the potent essence of your inner badass magic. Now, armed with this knowledge, you can catapult yourself into the multi-6 or 7-figure Soul-led empire.

I know it's a lot to digest. If you're bursting at the seams with a burning desire to scale your business and, like me, have a healthy dose of impatience, then I'm thrilled to offer you a shortcut. Together, we can compress the timeline from years of stumbling upon blind spots and unexpected energy leaks to just a few transformative months.

If you want to scale sustainably, aligned to your Soul Design Strategy, with a coach that truly understands your unique needs — my team and I would love to start the conversation: eugeniaoganova.com/start

Key Takeaways from Step 6 of The Conscious F.U.T.U.R.E. Method:

❖ **Scaling your business is the next frontier, achieved through the power of automation, assembling a dream team, and streamlined delivery.** To simplify scaling, avoid outsourcing from a place of fear or insecurity and focus on plugging leaks and elevating your operations.

❖ **To streamline your social media management, scheduling, and communication, a Virtual Assistant can navigate the pulse of your audience,** become your social media manager, and handle blog post and email scheduling. For multiple launches and automated sequences, video productions and social media events, an Online Business Manager (OBM) can help you orchestrate it all. **When hiring, ensure clarity on the desired actions, specificity of psychographics for required skills, and establish clear boundaries for communication and structure.**

- ❖ **Implement a well-structured client support system from the start, including thorough welcome emails, automated voice recordings, and personalized videos.** Pre-recorded video content for group programs guides clients, explains expectations, and addresses concerns. Offer specific content to navigate challenging phases and automate delivery to provide timely support. **Checkpoints to assess progress empower clients and showcase their growth.**
- ❖ **By structuring your client support system, integrating automation, pre-recorded content, and support coaches, you create a seamless and fulfilling experience.** Nurture warm leads through meaningful dialogue and empowering your virtual assistant with clear SOPs. Embrace automation to segment your list, create tailored email sequences, and lead prospects towards purchasing. The dance of nurture, follow-up conversations, and automation paves the way for scaling with grace, impact, and ease.

Chapter 8:

EMBODYING YOUR FUTURE IDENTITY

"I have not wasted my words on empty talk but have spoken only what is true; I have lived according to Maat."

– BOOK OF THE DEAD, 1550 BC, ANCIENT EGYPT

With the powerful tools and transformative strategies that I offer through the lens of business and Wealth Energetics, I feel compelled to dive deeper into this special aspect that can truly skyrocket your success. It's something I mentioned before, but its significance cannot be overstated.

It's time for the **Seven Sacred Rules of Soul Discipline.** These principles will guide you towards embodying the version of yourself who has already arrived at the pinnacle of your current desires and help you frictionlessly follow through on the strategies you've just learned about in Chapter 7 with unwavering determination to manifest your empire.

You now understand that to scale your business sustainably, a correct business strategy based on your Soul Design is needed. It must be paired with the use of non-linear Quantum Creation (which is coming in Part 3, Chapter 9).

Here's the secret: *You possess the extraordinary power to become anything you choose.* It all begins with a resolute DECISION — a declaration that reverberates through the depths of your Soul.

You have the authority to sculpt who you are BEING in order to do the right DOING — aka your identity, and it all starts with a single decision.

Merely attempting to modify your behavior or alter external circumstances is a futile endeavor. The key lies in a fundamental shift in who you ARE (in addition to implementing a correct strategy).

> To create what you want, you must make decisions and take aligned action (and you've learned the strategy for this in Chapter 7).

> To know *where* you are miscreating and **what** must change, you need to construct your Broadcast Chains (which is covered in the upcoming Chapter 9.)

> *To be able to do it* — have follow-through-power on your decisions without limit — you need these **non-negotiable Seven Sacred Rules** (which we are about to dive into!)

You must become HER — the one who has the power to move forward and do whatever is needed without friction, hardship, avoidance, doubt, or pressure.

It's time to look into HOW you became HER.

- ❖ Rule #1: Decide it is already done.
- ❖ Rule #2: Raise your Risk Factor.
- ❖ Rule #3: Doubt is always a Liar.
- ❖ Rule #4: Do what it takes until it takes.
- ❖ Rule #5: Become an Observer of Truth.
- ❖ Rule #6: I always get what I came for.
- ❖ Rule #7: I am always Abundant.

When my clients integrate these Seven Sacred Rules into their everyday reality, their path becomes frictionless, and their revenue multiplies. This is where Magic mates with Strategy and births mind-blowing outcomes!

I want to give you a chance, too, to embrace these Rules, my dear magical badass Leader, and step into *frictionless business.*

Rule #1: Decide it is Already Done

It all begins with your *relationship* with the Quantum field. It's about your ability to attune to the whispers of your Soul, discern its guidance, and distinguish it from the voice of fear. Trusting in the steps you are being shown is essential. You cannot deceive the Universe by merely going through the motions without undergoing internal transformation, just as daydreaming without taking action won't bring about the desired change.

What you truly desire is a trust-based relationship with the Universe, right? — The one that aligns with your unique Soul Design, rather than a pursuit-based mindset where you strive to reach a destination or become someone you are not.

The truth is you are already HER — your *Future Identity* exists as a different version of yourself within the Quantum field. *The key lies in embodying that specific resonance.*

> As a result of embracing this rule, your Vision is already manifesting — because, clearly, you have Quantum leaped onto the most perfect timeline.

> Your desired income has already been achieved — because, evidently, you have implemented the strategies aligned with your unique path, opening those magical "quantum doors."

> Your dream team is already here — because, of course, you have already magnetized the perfect support, both in the physical and non-physical realms.

This is where you release the need to constantly "figure it out" and strive to get there, because it is already done.

If you find yourself desperately seeking the way, it means you are resisting actually BEING there — where it is already accomplished in the Quantum field.

The truth is, **it is always** *already here.* You have the power to instantly shift into the new awareness where your desires already exist:

❖ You already exude confidence and know exactly what to say during that important presentation.
❖ You can already charge $20k for your offer, knowing your value and worth.
❖ You already lead an incredible team of support coaches that allows you to scale your business to 7-figures.

Embrace an unwavering belief that your desires have already materialized. *Align your Future Identity with the inevitability of your success — because she ALREADY possesses It.*

It is done.

You can choose to wait, or you can swiftly call it in, for it is already done.

The choice is yours.

Connect deeply with who you truly are, align with the flow of life, and step out of the way of your Soul so that God-Source can work through you. The result is being Spirit-led, where everything within you that is necessary will be utilized to make it happen.

This is how embodying your Future Identity (based on this Rule #1) creates the balance between taking correct action and being in tune with the divine flow of God-Source — so that you release the friction and leverage your uniqueness to manifest Wealth by Soul Design.

Rule #2: Raise your Risk Factor

Now let's look into decision-making, the other major self-sabotage place! If you find yourself taking forever to make a decision, or feeling indecisive, it's a sign that you're not fully aligned with your Soul Design — and this can seriously hold you back in your business. The reason it's so hard is because your lizard brain wants you to stick to what you know, even if it's not serving you or helping you grow (your Reticular Activating System (RAS) is a network of neurons that look for similarities even if they will make you miserable and keep you stuck under 6-figures working way too hard!). The good news is that your higher brain function, which is connected to your Soul, wants you to take risks and evolve.

So, what's your risk factor?

The speed and clarity of your decision-making is directly related to your perceived risk tolerance.

One way to test this is to ask yourself, "If I lost [insert material input here], how much would my life really change? How worried would I be?" The answer to this question will give you an idea of how much fear is blocking your decision-making process.

For me, I've learned to have a high-risk tolerance — losing X amount of dollars or clients (even if it's all I have!) wouldn't terrify me because I know I am capable and tenacious, and I know how and what to do to create it all over again. This is why I'm able to make fast decisions without worrying.

No one's Soul Design is to be indecisive!

Worry and fear are just personal insecurities that hold you back from your full potential. It's time to break free from the conditioning that there is only "one right answer" that you need to find to succeed. In reality, there are endless possibilities and timelines in the Quantum field, and you have infinite chances to get it right.

Making a decision based on your Soul Design Strategy, trusting that the Universe will course-correct you along the way, and implementing these corrections, is how your business skyrockets.

When you're in motion, your energy guides can help you manifest your desired outcome by course-correcting. But if you're standing still, waiting for the perfect answer to drop into your lap, they can't help you.

Consistently increasing your risk-tolerance is a huge part of leadership and any highly successful personal brand. In fact, I would love for you to adopt a new axiom: Worry is a waste of energy! Understanding how you're meant to make decisions based on your unique Soul Design *eliminates friction of worry*, so you don't override your fear, you resolve it.

Rule #3: Doubt is Always a Liar

Doubt, oh doubt, the favorite companion of self-sabotage. It's only natural for doubt and insecurity to be woven into the fabric of our human experience. But here's a moment of truth for you... YOU, my dear, are absolutely freaking awesome! (And yes, there's a point to this, just wait).

I remember from about 10 years ago this profound conversation with the Solar Council, a group of 10D energy beings I've been blessed to work with for ages. In that moment, as doubt tried to dim my divine certainty, they hit me with a powerful question:

"Can you not see your immense magnificence?"

And in that instant, I felt it. I felt the radiance of my own phenomenality, despite the lingering presence of doubt. It was then that I started asking potential clients on my application form, "How awesome are you?" And let me tell you, it has become an extraordinary filter for attracting my ideal clients! When I read responses like, "I am a 100% awesome goddess!" or "I am a badass rebel ready to conquer the world!" or even "I am a cool, non-human, freaking fantastic being!", I know that I've found my soulmate clients. And, my dear Leader, deep within you, you know you've got that magnificent spark too! ☺

Now, let me introduce you to a new rule: *Doubt is always a liar.*

Whenever doubt sneaks in, acknowledge its presence, and if necessary, explore its roots. But never, ever believe it to be true. Because it never is.

What does this mean?

Yes, the lies of your fears and doubts will still try to taunt you, but once you embrace your new Future Identity, you no longer fuel them with your energy. You decide that you are awesome, eternally and unconditionally, and as a result, you effortlessly create everything in alignment with your Soul, with ease, flow, and without any friction.

It also means that those parents who may have hurt you (or your body!), those teachers who misunderstood you, those clients who resist doing the work, or that team that doesn't always listen — it's all part of a story that can trigger your anger and project past pain. But my dear, it's all a lie.

Let's face it, hurt tends to be contagious, right? And hurt people often end up hurting others. No one achieves a 7-figure empire without transcending some serious shit! You have the power to be compassionate towards yourself and others without bypassing or allowing people to trample over your boundaries.

Furthermore, you no longer need to prove yourself. Doubt is ALWAYS a liar. You are not defined by your past mistakes, karmic patterns, or parental conditioning. You were born worthy. Your passion and deep desire to shift human consciousness have a profound purpose. It's time to unhook yourself from the hypnotic illusion of doubt.

When you align with your Soul Design and Mission, you stop surrendering your power to doubt and embrace the unshakeable truth that you are a Leader.

You become unfuckwithable!

In this alignment, NOTHING can touch you, time collapses, and you manifest 7-figures effortlessly. You become the embodiment of Maat, the Ancient Egyptian concept of "Divine Truth."

Embrace your awesomeness, dear Leader, and become unfuckwithable, for doubt holds no power over you when you step into the truth of who you truly are.

Rule #4: Do What It Takes Until It Takes

This is one of the most crucial rules there is, where manifestation moves from multi-D into linear 3D. This is where you get over yourself and it all gets done!

Oh, and let me tell you, it's a rule that can stir lots of resistance, especially for spiritual coaches and healers.

This is the Follow Through on Decision rule.

Resistance slinks in like a cunning saboteur, fueled by your emotional waves based on conditioned responses to life.

Picture this: your parents insisted you play the cello, a wretched instrument that clashed with your very Soul. And now, in your business, you rebel against anything that smacks of consistency and gradual progress, haunted by memories of those dreaded cello lessons. Instead of building a solid marketing strategy and repurposing content, you find yourself trapped on the content creation rollercoaster, your income swinging between feast and famine. When you're shown how to create content that converts, an emotional knee-jerk reaction screams, "I shouldn't have to do this!" And so, you unwittingly sabotage your marketing efforts, leaving you to toil even harder to sell your offers.

Or perhaps your schoolteacher constantly berated your messy homework, while your parents showered praise only upon your perfect grades. Now, your business remains stuck because you can't birth anything unless it meets impossible standards of perfection. Each time you're urged to show up with your most authentic message, sheer terror grips you, fearing judgment and rejection. Consequently, you push yourself to the brink, accumulating certifications, crafting meticulously produced videos, and rigidly adhering to every strategy. The pressure mounts, and before you know it, you despise the very essence of your business.

Resistance, my dear, is the dream killer.

Unless you grasp the art of taking action in spite of resistance, your dreams lie dormant — lifeless and unfulfilled. There will be no next-level clients, no overflowing programs, no 7-figure empire, and certainly no passage through the mystical "Quantum doors." None of it.

Beware the deceptive seduction of "but I don't want to..." — it masquerades as "It doesn't feel aligned" or "I'm just not feeling inspired" or "The energy isn't right." But beneath those words lies a torrent of emotional reactions rooted in past discomfort. Fear is NOT a stop sign, it means "proceed with caution" but proceed nevertheless!

When you make a DECISION — you must FOLLOW THROUGH.

If you find yourself unable or unwilling to follow through due to these emotional reactions, you are firmly entrenched in past conditioning. In doing so, you send a message to the Universe that you are not trustworthy, not the master, and that you are unavailable to manifest your grand Vision.

And so, nothing manifests.

Soul Discipline, my dear conscious Leader, is *the art of giving yourself a command and steadfastly adhering to it.* It is the embodiment of self-discipline where the power of choice resides. No external authority figures discipline you — it is *you* who chooses to follow through on your decisions.

What does it feel like to embody Sacred Rule #4?

It means making a decision and forging ahead, regardless of emotional reactions, negative thoughts, doubts and fears, or bodily sensations.

The choice you make dictates your actions, not how you feel, not the level of discomfort, not your circumstances, not the people from your past who wounded you, not your current clients, not those who rejected you, not even the actions of others — none of it.

Now, this rule is not about restriction or lack; it is about embracing the abundance of choice and mastering the art of doing what it takes, until it takes. When you say "I don't want...", it is steeped in fear of discomfort, as outlined in Rule #2. It signifies that your Lower Self has taken the reins. But when you wholeheartedly embrace Sacred Rule #4, you stop *tolerating* this.

By embodying this powerful rule, you liberate yourself from the battle against imaginary authority figures. No more rebelling against what is truly good for you. You see, dear badass Leader, you don't "have to" do anything — you GET TO do it because you have made a conscious decision.

You simply show up and do what it takes until it takes. There is no emotional charge around it, no friction.

Rule #5: Become an Observer of Truth

One of the most important aspects of personal growth is the ability to witness the events of your life and business without being consumed by the drama. When we forget to observe, we become entangled in the experience, and our emotions can undermine our progress. Let's face it, those emotions stem from your Lower Self — the part of you that has been shaped by parental influences, societal expectations, ancestral patterns, and past karma. This is precisely why taking control of your self-definition and showing up as your Future Identity is the pathway to unlocking Wealth by your Soul Design.

At the core of all friction lies worry — the worry of being too much or too little, too similar or too different, too structured or too flexible, and so on. Worry signifies a lack of PRESENCE in the moment, stretching your energy across the linear timeline (trapping you in 3D and outside of the Quantum Creation). While we acknowledge the importance of having a vision and a strategic plan, if you find yourself overly immersed in participation, you'll be tossed around like a leaf in a raging river.

Step back and assume the role of an observer, embodying a state of detached wisdom. Cultivate a higher perspective that empowers you to navigate challenges with grace and clarity.

We must recognize that significant manifestations are meant to flow through us from the divine God-Source. We're not here to play small — this is important work, and deep down, you know it. Are you willing to serve as the conduit? Are you willing to eliminate the unnecessary drama and perceive the purity of the message for what it truly is?

The Truth *is*... yeap... it just IS.

When you observe, you can discern lies for what they are, allowing you to recognize and embrace the Truth, the divine Maat, amidst it all. You can see the lessons. You can identify the solutions. You know what your prospects need to hear to join you. You know how to guide your clients towards success. You know who you are and *remain fully present in that Truth, even amidst the conditioned lies that accompany the human experience.*

Rule #6: I Always Get What I Came For

In the realm of expectations, there exists a powerful truth: *you will receive exactly what you seek.* The Universe, in its cosmic symphony, conspires to align with your desires, ensuring that every experience and encounter carries a divine purpose, propelling you closer to your dreams.

Consider this Rule, bearing the same unwavering energy as Rule #3 (Doubt is always a Liar), yet centered on your interactions with the environment and others. In Rule #3, we focused on embracing your inherent greatness and dismissing the voice of doubt. Here, in Rule #6, we trust that the Universe, alongside fellow beings, will deliver. It's an unwavering expectation that others will show up and fulfill their roles, while you learn valuable lessons and attain what you need. Rest assured; your needs shall always be met.

❖ Expect everyone on your sales calls already convinced of the value you offer, trusting you implicitly — and witness it becoming a reality.

❖ Expect your clients to experience astounding results — and witness their triumphs.

❖ Envision yourself skillfully unraveling challenging situations — and emerge victorious.

❖ Expect that the coach you signed up with will catalyze a life-altering transformation, regardless of her words or actions, simply because you have decided so — and witness your business flourish under her guidance.

Do you see? It's not a mere demand for the Universe to gratify your Ego's whims; instead, it's about being Soul-led and attracting what aligns with your unique Soul Design. And let me assure you, there is no Soul Design out there that doesn't include access to Wealth!

Yet, when this Sacred Rule is overlooked, you unwittingly fall back into expecting what life has always presented you based on past experiences, traumas, and conditioning. When things don't unfold as desired, you push harder: "Let me just finish this sales page", "One more DM — maybe she'll buy", "Hire another team member, that'll solve it". Sounds familiar?

But in doing so, you transition into a state of striving (see Rule #1), driven by a lack of trust that your needs will be fulfilled.

The reason you may not be attracting the clients, money, or ease you desire is because a part of you has already decided you're unworthy of such blessings. Remember, we always receive what we expect.

Thus, *if you're not receiving what you desire, it serves as universal feedback that you must recalibrate your expectation frequency.*

However, there's no need for self-blame or self-criticism. Instead, become an explorer of your inner landscape, correct your energy broadcast, reshape your Future Identity, and reassess your expectations.

Why? Because **what you energize ultimately manifests.**

I'll illustrate this concept with a metaphor one of my coaches uses: Imagine your job is to cut down trees, but your axe is rusty. Most women approach their businesses in a similar manner: fueled by a few shots of tequila (to num the friction pain), blindfolded (due to lack of aligned business strategy), and wearing stilettos for added excitement (making it harder than it has to be), they swing their rusty axe vigorously at trees they can't see. This is the *"I'm doing everything I can, why isn't it working?"* approach. Seriously girl, stop!

While action remains crucial, I invite you to pause and invoke the Sacred Rule #6 "I always get what I came for." Tune into your innermost being, *listen to your Soul, and witness how the divine speaks through your Soul Design, sharpening your axe* and revealing the shortcuts. Only then, with expectations aligned and in perfect harmony, should you proceed to take action. This creates efficient and effective action where no effort or energy is wasted.

This is one of my personal expectations: "I am divinely guided to shortcuts". And indeed, I am, for I expect nothing less.

- ❖ You expect joy, ease, and fulfillment — and get it.
- ❖ You expect yourself to have powerful mind-blowing results — and you do!
- ❖ You expect amazing clients to come into your world and invest large sums of money without drama — and they gracefully do.
- ❖ You expect to double or triple your income — and why the hell not?!

However, let's not forget the "fine print" from the Universe: these expectations must be coupled with the appropriate business strategy tailored to your unique circumstances and implemented consistently.

When you consistently channel your energy through expectation and reinforce it by embodying your Future Identity, you are finally broadcasting your intentions at the frequency of Quantum Wealth. You are directing all your energy towards the place in the Quantum field where your vision dwells, and thus manifestation becomes inevitable.

If you want to collapse time and arrive at your next level — multi-6 or 7-figures in a sustainable way — then this Rule #6 is extremely important. Let go of the "I'll believe it when I see it" mentality, which places the burden of proof on the Universe before you show up at the correct frequency or take the necessary steps.

It is the other way around: you get to be who you were born to be, embody your Future Identity, and wholeheartedly engage in actions aligned with your Soul Design Strategy NOW.

And *EXPECT the Quantum field to respond by manifesting your desires*, for you have become a perfect match.

Because, my dear, Maat — the Divine Truth — is, just is. The real problem lies in your lack of conscious decision-making regarding your very identity. You see, it's all within you, for this grand game of life is simply a dance of possibilities. You hold the power to be whoever you desire to be, to embody your Future Identity, as you boldly step into the magnificent essence of your God-given uniqueness.

Embracing this truth and anchoring your Soul Design is a game changer, my dear, a revelation that transforms your market positioning and client attraction into a joyful playground of infinite possibilities.

Rule #7: I am Always Abundant

Let's clean up the massive self-sabotage that is scarcity energetics. You know, that insidious little voice in your head whispering, "I'm not sure if I'm good enough," even as you bask in the glory of amazing testimonials and already multiple 6 figures! Or perhaps it taunts you with thoughts like, "They won't pay a premium for my offer," or "Where in the world can I find those high-ticket clients?" It's that scarcity mindset, rooted deep in the soil of lack.

But fear not, for I have a Rule to help you liberate yourself from this confining mindset — always vibrating at the Quantum Wealth frequency.

First, if you're here on this path, manifesting great results for your clients with your superpowers, then my dear, you are worth every damn bit of it. You are more than enough exactly as you are. The rest is a matter of making a bold decision, devising a Soul Design Strategy, and unapologetically following through (see Rule #4).

And let me tell you something fierce: your dream clients are not lost in the abyss. Oh no, they are right here. And trust me when I say they would willingly throw their credit cards your way if they could truly grasp the incredible value you bring to their lives.

Now, let's talk about the wild world of social media. If you're selling your magic on Facebook, then guess what? Your ideal clients are hanging there! Or maybe they're sipping lattes on Instagram or mingling on LinkedIn. The point is, my dear, they are wherever YOU choose to be. So claim this rule — I am always abundant, embrace your platform of choice, and watch as your Soul-aligned clients come flocking to you like moths to a captivating flame. (Also, Chapter 7 adds marketing strategies to this).

Here's the ultimate truth bomb that'll make your Soul quiver with excitement:

there is no lack, only pure, unlimited abundance.

Your supply is infinite, boundless, and immeasurable. Everything you desire, everything that sets your Soul ablaze, is already here, right within your grasp.

The very fact that you desire something means it's calling out to you, ready to be materialized in all its glory.

You see, in the realm of infinite possibilities, *what you yearn for already exists in the Quantum field.* It's a mesmerizing dance of interconnectedness, a universal law known as Quantum Entanglement.

Let's say, you crave an influx of $100k gracefully flowing into your account within four weeks. And to top it off, you dream of working with a handful of soulmate clients, radiating abundance from every pore, who joyfully invest $20k in your transformative program. Well, my dear Leader, hold onto your glittering crown, because those people are already right beside you, waiting to embark on this sacred journey with you. Can you feel them?

It's all part of the grand tapestry of the Universal Law of Quantum Entanglement.
❖ Can you feel it?
❖ Will you wholeheartedly embrace this truth?
❖ Choose to make this Sacred Rule your guiding star, unwavering in the face of any emotional waves, mental illusions, or karmic obstacles that dare to cross your path?

There is ONLY abundance. "Lack" is nothing more than a human-created illusion, a mirage in the desert of limitless possibilities.

If your heart yearns for a mind-boggling $200k or $500k live launch, believe with every fiber of your being that it already exists, dancing tantalizingly within reach in the vast expanse of the Quantum field, just waiting for you to materialize it into your reality.

And that $100k client you crave? Oh, my dear, she's already a member of your audience, patiently waiting for you to align with the frequency of Wealth that will magnetically draw her to you.

And let's not forget those amazing opportunities you envision, like being interviewed at that illustrious event or podcast, even if you haven't yet crossed paths with the host. Fear not, dear friend, for the door to that very opportunity is already ajar, beckoning you to step through it. It exists, and if your vibrational energy resonates with it, you can effortlessly glide into that interview and bask in the spotlight. It's all here for you, awaiting your command.

This Sacred Rule — "I am Always Abundant" — is the essence of vibrating at a Quantum Wealth frequency.

It's not a mere intellectual concept; it's a sacred state of being. In this realm, the shackles of lack crumble to dust, and miracles are the norm.

But beware, Leader, for if you allow daily thoughts of lack to permeate your reality, you shatter the delicate equilibrium of the Quantum Wealth frequency where true magic unfolds. This is where Soul Discipline becomes your steadfast ally, supporting you in embodying the truth of abundance and banishing scarcity from your consciousness. (See Sacred Rule #4)

So, magical rebel Leader, align yourself with the Quantum Wealth frequency so that your desires transform into tangible manifestations. The miracles are not distant dreams; they are an integral part of your divine birthright. When you immerse yourself in the frequency of limitless possibilities, you witness the supernatural and extraordinary unfold before your very eyes.

It's time to unleash your inherent power and create a reality that dances to the rhythm of your Soul. This is truly Wealth by Soul Design.

Part 3:

MANIFESTING QUANTUM LEAPS

"Not by might nor by power, but by My Spirit"

– BOOK OF ZECHARIAH, CHAPTER 4, VERSE 6

Dear badass rebel Leader! Now that I've shared all the juicy details of my framework, it's time to dive into something crucial for your mind-blowing success: the fusion of rock-solid linear business strategies, which we've covered extensively in Part 2, with the mind-bending awesomeness of non-linear Quantum Creation (here in Part 3). Brace yourself for a journey unlike any other!

Let's dive straight into the truth: we hold the power to make the impossible possible, to create magic, to tap into the supernatural. Miracles aren't reserved for a select few deemed worthy by a higher power. We ARE the higher power when we live in alignment with our Soul Design Strategy.

One of the most prevalent reasons why so many coaches either don't end up with a profitable business, or fail to scale their crazy-busy business, is the inner turmoil that arises when it's time to risk, show up, and shine. *Fear, doubt, and anxiety rear their ugly heads, casting shadows.*

You might find yourself ensnared in an endless cycle of self-analysis, perpetually processing your issues. Or never fully embrace the correct business and marketing strategies nor step into the magnificent Future Identity that beckons you. Perhaps you're plagued by self-sabotage, continuously hindering your progress? Or falling prey to your own conditioning, you might be trapped in over-achieving, putting endless pressure on yourself to succeed at all costs.

All of these issues have one thing in common: it feels like it will take forever to get to the outcome you want. And that feels "hard".

Now, let me share with you the incredible transformations I've witnessed in my clients' businesses when they adopt *my methodology of merging solid linear business strategies with non-linear Quantum Creation.* It's trendy to talk about "quantum leaps" these days, but most people don't truly understand what it means. Supernatural abilities are inherent in our nature as Souls, and a true Quantum leap is not just a change in circumstances, but a shift to a whole new personal REALITY.

I've seen my clients…
❖ Jump from giving her expertise away for free — to effortlessly selling four $7k packages in 4 months.
❖ Struggle to sell a severely underpriced offer to wrong clients — to selling $5k offer on repeat to the perfect clients in just 3 months.

- ❖ Step out of feeling frazzled and overwhelmed, never feeling quite in control of what was happening — straight into peace, clarity, and certainty in a month.
- ❖ Leap from not even having a high-ticket offer and thinking it'll take years to get one to work — to market-testing and selling their first ever $15k offer — in 2 months!
- ❖ Shift from endless launches of new offers — into excited about selling one signature offer and creatively sharing with her community.
- ❖ Graduate from posting all the time on social media, not knowing what to write about, and being totally stressed — to only saying what's needed — no stress, lots of conversions.
- ❖ Leap from a false reality of frustrating sales calls with unqualified prospects — to a beautiful new reality of a pre-sold audience who loves her offer.

How, you ask?

How can you make these magical leaps too?

By aligning all your Quantum ducks in a row. And there are two key elements to making the supernatural happen.

> Firstly, you need to **consciously use the Quantum Creation process** in your business. This means getting crystal clear on what you are broadcasting, tapping into the energy of the Universe, and expanding your Wealth capacity to receive your miracles. This way, you co-create your desired reality — while being masterful of your own resonance.

> Secondly, you need to **embody a correct Future Identity**. It means that you need to live, breathe and act as though you have already manifested your miracles. Because when you do, you're sending a clear message to the Universe that you are who you claim you are, and you're ready to receive

all the amazing opportunities, clients and synchronicities that are waiting for you.

So, dear rebel Leader, it's time to step into your power and start *predictably creating your own miracles.* Using my methodology, you'll have the tools, the knowledge, and the energy — so you can go out there and create it. Because let's face it — you were born to live a miraculous life!

In the next chapters, I'll unpack for you these parts of my methodology that will anchor Quantum Creation and your Future Identity into practical components. I'll help you take the first steps to reducing the energy friction that makes everything feel so hard, so you can uplevel your business into multi-6 or 7-figures without pressure or forcing yourself into unnatural strategies, using SUPERNATURAL!

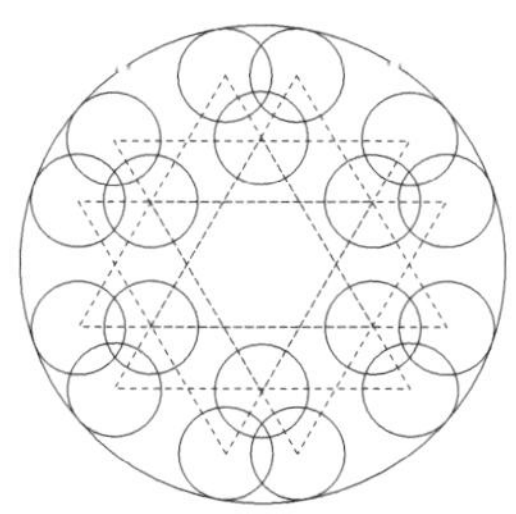

Chapter 9:

MASTERING THE QUANTUM CREATION PROCESS

"The future is not fixed; it is in your own hands. To do the best for it is the truest prudence."

- ZARATHUSTRA, PERSIA, 13TH CENTURY BC

Let me tell you, my beautiful friend, about the power of *Quantum Creation* and why you absolutely need to care about it! Because when you're able to harness this incredible force to your advantage, you'll experience some seriously magical transformations in your business and beyond. Here's what I'm talking about:

1. *You'll make Quantum leaps in your business* — instead of slowly inching your way forward, you'll jump ahead with incredible speed and grace, aligned with your Soul Design Strategy.

2. *You'll start attracting opportunities that might have been INVISIBLE to you before* — these are the "Quantum doors" that will lead you to your new personal reality. And when you

open those doors and walk through them, you'll be amazed at what you're able to achieve.

3. *Best of all, you'll feel like there's no friction* — everything will flow smoothly inside of you. You'll know exactly what needs to be done, and you'll just do it. It's an incredible feeling, and it's all thanks to the power of Quantum Creation.

In my Conscious F.U.T.U.R.E. Mastery program, I dive into the multiple layers of this concept, but let's keep it practical here. Later, in this Chapter, I will share with you a very cool bonus: a practical exercise I use to guide my high-level clients that can totally fix your manifestation capacity!

To get the most from the bonus exercise, you'll want to understand the lay of the land first. The material 3D reality we operate in follows the rules of physics, cause-and-effect, linear time, and step-by-step growth. However, this reality is just a mental construct, and our minds are conditioned to believe that this is all there is.

In truth, this is just one layer of perception among many. *If you want ease, flow, magic, and wealth, it's much easier to access them by utilizing the laws outside of this 3D mental construct.* (Did I tell you I'm not a typical business coach?)

The reality outside of this mental construct is what we call **Quantum Reality**. It's the unrealized potential, and different rules apply. Here, you have the power to DETERMINE your reality.

Hey, do you know about the Double-slit Experiment that proved this?

It's a classic illustration of how things can be both waves (unrealized potential) and particles (manifested reality) in Quantum Mechanics. Thomas Young first did it in 1801, but John Wheeler took it up again in 1979 to study how consciousness affects the collapse of the wave function. Turns out, our minds are a big part of what creates reality!

In the experiment, they shot waves at a wall with two slits and observed which particles went through which slit. The wild thing is, when someone was watching, the results matched what that person expected or felt. That means reality was all in a neutral "wave" state until somebody had an opinion about it.

Basically, everything starts as unrealized potential, and we're the ones who turn it into manifested particles with our perception. So, the Quantum Laws of Creation work totally different from the material physical laws we're used to. Cool, huh?

- ❖ In the Quantum realm, your Identity determines the resonance you broadcast.
- ❖ This resonance is then translated into beliefs, thoughts, emotions, and actions that shape your reality.
- ❖ The Law of Resonance states that the Universe responds to this frequency, not to your desires, thoughts, or words. The Universe speaks Frequency, and it responds to the energy you are broadcasting.
- ❖ And here is the kicker — if you are not getting what you want, it's likely because what you're putting out is *different* from what you actually desire.

For example, you're on a sales call with a prospect who is an ideal fit for your offer. As you eagerly hope for them to sign up, a subtle undercurrent of insecurity surfaces within you, whispering doubts like, "Am I truly capable of helping someone of her caliber? What if she sees through me and discovers I'm a fraud?" This sneaky manifestation of Imposter Syndrome reveals a hidden desire to hide, to avoid being exposed as an imposter. And in a twist of fate, the prospect begins raising objections and eventually exits the call without committing. You see, my conflicted friend, your fear-based desire held more power than your conscious desire, resulting in a missed opportunity.

This is precisely why gaining awareness of the energy you transmit to the Universe is paramount for successful manifestation.

And now, dear Leader, let's explore the true nature of your energetic broadcasts.

Here we go, you're about to have a quick win, a potent key to unlocking your Quantum reality and effortlessly attracting those coveted high-ticket clients. Brace yourself, for this is the first and often most challenging step on your path to greatness. It all begins with a simple yet profound awareness. Embrace the truth that this very awareness is what sets in motion the magnificent unfolding of your desires, and that by tapping into this power, you unleash a divine flow and momentum that propels you towards your goals with grace and ease.

To align your broadcast with your Soul desires, you need to lay out your *broadcast chain* and see what you're truly putting out into the Universe. *It's a key step in mastering the Quantum Creation process and manifesting your desires effortlessly.* The progression of manifestation process from Quantum into 3D is what we call a "broadcast chain" in my methodology:

Identity > Beliefs > Thoughts > Emotions > Actions > Reality

If you're anything like me, you want a shortcut. Not that we don't enjoy the scenery, but enough already, right?! I've got you: here are 3 axioms that will change the game for your manifestation skills:

1. The Quantum field is overflowing with possibilities: 100% possible 100% of the time. But, the catch is, it's all in the unrealized state until you bring it into being.
2. Your Identity, beliefs, thoughts, and emotions are *filters* that determine what is possible for YOU specifically. Your Story, the meaning you give to experiences, creates these filters. Whatever you believe is not possible for you, is not possible because your filter blocks it.
3. Your body and actions are the anchor for creation, which means that what your anchor can hold (aka what you embody) is what you can create.

So, let's say you want to make 7-figures this year, but your filter says, *"hell no, that means I'll have to work too hard and be stressed AF."* Well, guess what? Your anchor/body freaks out, and your Wealth capacity shrinks. You just blocked the timeline where you could have made those 7-figures, even if you had the right strategy, offer, audience, and sales steps. See? *It's all about the interference pattern you create with your thoughts and beliefs.*

But, if you're aligned with your Identity, beliefs, thoughts, and emotions, then your Wealth capacity expands, and you're open to receive without having to know how. For example, let's say you want to do a live launch for your offer, and you need 3 well-connected people to promote it. You don't know who these people are, but you're holding the idea of them coming into your life. Lo and behold, 3 people show up — one invites you to her podcast and offers to promote your launch, the second is an old acquaintance who wants to help, and the third is a client referral who has over 100K Instagram followers in your niche. It worked, even though there was no logical explanation for it.

To summarize: to create anything, your *filter* must perceive it as a possibility and your anchor has to be able to hold it. If either one of these doesn't work, then it's not a possibility for your reality, thus the desired outcome cannot manifest.

- ❖ The OLD broadcast chain: **Reality > Actions > Emotions > Thoughts > Beliefs > old Identity**
- ❖ The NEW broadcast chain: **new Identity > Beliefs > Thoughts > Emotions > Actions > Reality**

Now it's time to grab your journal and a pen, get cozy, and let's dive into your broadcast so we can fix your manifestation capacity! These prompts are the same ones I use to guide my high-level clients, so get ready to dig deep.

To get the most out of this exercise, focus on one specific thing at a time. I typically have my clients do around 20 of these chains on all aspects of the problem they're facing. By honing in on small aspects, you'll be able to identify patterns and repetitions that show you the larger issue and where you need to make corrections.

So, let's get started! Ask yourself these questions:

1. What's the current problem you're experiencing? Is it feeling overworked and too busy? Struggling to communicate with high-ticket clients? Feeling unsupported or micromanaging your clients and team? Something else? *(be specific, focus on one aspect)*
2. What actions are you taking (or avoiding) because of this problem?
3. What habitual emotional reactions do you find yourself having?
4. What habitual thoughts come up for you around this problem?
5. What do you believe as the character inside this story?
6. As that character, what story are you telling yourself over and over about the situation?
7. What role are you currently playing inside this story?
8. What's another role you could play that would feel stronger, more aligned, and more abundant? *(Think of it as a counterweight or an upgrade).*
9. If you were playing that new role, how would the story change?
10. What would you naturally believe if you were that character?
11. What thoughts would you be having?
12. What emotions would you feel habitually?
13. And what actions would you take?
14. Finally, what would your external reality look like in that new role?

Let's look at one of the examples … we'll call her Emily.

Emily's problem was that her business was tremendously complicated. She kept creating new offers, which forced her to make new marketing campaigns and sales pages for each new offer, never being satisfied with any of them. She was stuck in a cycle of boredom, frustration, and insecurity, constantly asking herself, "What is wrong with me?" "Why is this so hard?", and "How will I fill this new program?" She believed that focusing on one offer would kill her creativity.

This was a part of a larger story that she would become trapped in if she chose any one thing — because what if it was the wrong thing!? Emily had been playing the role of Rebel for most of her life, which on the outside may have looked cool and brazen but left behind a trail of failed relationships and business ventures, along with a deep sense of insecurity and bitterness.

Emily's transformation began with the Zoom call. She knew she needed help and so she put her fears aside and reached out. Together, we got straight to the root of the problem — Emily's Rebel role. Rather than exploring her childhood and other personal transformation work she had already done, we simply decided to shift her main role to the counterweight: *the Creatrix*. This was in total alignment with Emily' archetypes: Artist and Romantic. Emily immediately felt that this was her divine destiny, her whole body vibrated when she allowed herself to BECOME Creatrix — she felt it to her bones, her DNA, her Soul, it was right, it resonated to her core.

As a Creatrix, Emily was inspired and believed that there was always a place for her creativity without any limitations. She shifted her thoughts to questions like "How can I explain this more creatively?" and "What new event can I create to promote my signature offer?" Instead of feeling bored and frustrated, she fell in love with her life and had fun with her work. She felt excited, certain of her worth, and open to receiving abundance. Her actions became aligned with her intuitive knowing and creative flow, she began effortlessly putting out various new free events — all promoting her one offer. Emily's life changed: she no longer felt friction in her business, rebelling against the world — her signature offer sold well, and she didn't need to constantly create new ones. Her creative energy was fully expressed in the marketing through new live events and the delivery of her signature offer.

Emily did her broadcast chains over 30 times to finally get to the place where the Identity was revealed. Here are her final (summarized from the 30 she did) broadcast chains clarified:

❖ The OLD broadcast chain:
Overcomplicated business **(old Reality)** > creating new offers, new marketing campaigns, new sales pages for each new offer (Actions) > boredom, frustration, dissatisfaction, insecurity (Emotions) > "What is wrong with me?" "Why is this so hard?", "How will I fill this new program?" (Thoughts) > trapped if she chose any one thing (Belief) > Rebel **(old Identity)**

❖ The NEW broadcast chain:
Creatrix **(new Identity)** > there is always a place for creativity without any limitations (Belief) > "How can I explain this more creatively?" and "What new event can I create to promote my signature offer?" (Thoughts) > excited, certain of her worth, and open to receiving abundance (Emotions) > monthly new free events promoting one offer (Actions) > no friction in her business, signature offer sold well, fully expressed creatively in the marketing through new live events **(new Reality)**

Doing these broadcast chains many times for all aspects of the ONE major problem (touching on various sub-problems related to it) will get you to the root. Take some time to reflect on your answers and see what patterns emerge. As you write up many broadcast chains about the same problem (bottom-up from

Reality to old Identity and top-down new Identity to new Reality), the answers in the 3 categories closer to the top (Belief/Story/Identity) become the same — this means you got to the root.

Like Emily, you would also do this many times considering all aspects of the problem you're having to zero in on the root. By identifying the root of the problem and shifting your Identity, you'll be able to align yourself with your Soul Design Strategy and manifest the reality you desire. You've got this!

Now, it's your turn. Remember the 5 questions you journaled on a bit earlier? To help you, here is a cheat-sheet that you can fill out using these answers:

My problem is ______________, and I am doing/avoid doing ___________ , making me feel ________________, ________________, and ______________. My daily thoughts rotate around ________________, ________________, and ______________. I know that my Higher Self knows better, but my Lower Self fully believes ______________, ______________, and ______________. This is a part of my larger habitual story that I ________________, where underneath it all I ultimately feel ______________.

Inside this story, I am ______________. This is the role I play in my life many times before, it affects my life by ______________, ______________, and ______________.

The NEW role I choose from now on is ________________. Being her, my new story is ___________ and she believes ______________. Her habitual thoughts are ______________, ______________, and ______________. Every day she feels ______________, ______________, and ______________. She takes ________________ action with ease and alignment, and her world looks like ____________________________.

Let's summarize this into two major broadcast chains — old and new — using the data you've gathered:

> ❖ The OLD broadcast chain:
> ________ *Old Reality* > ________ *Actions* > ________ *Emotions* > ________ *Thoughts* > ________ *Beliefs* > ________ *Old Identity.*
>
> ❖ The NEW broadcast chain:
> ________ *New Identity* > ________ *Beliefs* > ________ *Thoughts* > ________ *Emotions* > ________ *Actions* > ________ *New Reality.*

Here's another example of a typical client — let's call her Nina.

She also began her journey to a scalable business with one choice — to email my team. She joined my Conscious F.U.T.U.R.E. Mastery program and one of the first things we did was these broadcast chains. She did many, just like you, to get to the main overall ones that show her the Identity shift required. This is what is looked like:

❖ The OLD broadcast chain:
Can't attract ideal high-ticket clients, who she attracts are wrong people **(old Reality)** > posting on social media, networking on Facebook and LinkedIn, tried to uplevel sales copy, handles challenging clients (Actions) > overwhelmed, constant pressure, fears burnout (Emotions) > "What am I missing?", "Why is this so hard?", "Where do I find high-ticket clients?" (Thoughts) > answers are outside, find right answer and exert massive effort, success will follow (Belief) > Follower **(old Identity)**

❖ The NEW broadcast chain:
Leader **(new Identity)** > all answers are within, there is only HER unique strategy (Belief) > "If I knew the answer, what would it be?", "What message wants to come out of me?", "How can I lead in

this conversation?" (Thoughts) > confident, present, fully aligned (Emotions) > shares only three purposeful and aligned posts per week, magnetizing messaging (Actions) > many sales calls only with ideal clients **(new Reality)**

See it? Let's put this into sentences so it's easier to see the flow:

Nina's problem is that she struggles to attract high-ticket clients for her amazing offer, even though she has plenty of interest. However, most of the prospects she encounters are either the wrong fit or cannot afford her services. She puts in consistent effort by regularly posting on social media, showing up in various Facebook groups, and networking on LinkedIn. She constantly tweaks her tagline, changes her sales copy, and spends hours dealing with challenging clients, wishing she could just focus on coaching. Despite all her hard work, the desired results seem to elude her. Nina feels overwhelmed by the constant pressure she puts on herself to be fully booked with ideal clients and worries about burnout. Her thoughts revolve around questions like "What am I missing?", "Why is this so hard?", and "Where do I find high-ticket clients?" She believes that if she could just find the right formula and exert massive effort, success will follow. This is part of a larger story where she looks for external answers, and she finds herself playing the role of the Follower.

Instead of exploring her past issues, which Nina has already extensively worked on over the years, we immediately shift her identity to the opposite: the Leader. Nina is the Ruler and Explorer archetypes, so this made sense on so many levels. This transformation brings Nina an immediate sense of relief, as she intuitively knows that she is meant to embody this role rather than hiding behind strategies and tactics that don't resonate with her.

As a Leader, Nina recognizes that the answers she seeks lie within herself. This conviction is no longer just a mental understanding;

it becomes a deep inner knowing. She realizes that there is no one-size-fits-all strategy — there is only HER unique strategy. Nina embarks on a journey of uncovering her own path in marketing, and her thoughts now become filled with empowering questions like "If I knew the answer, what would it be?", "What message wants to come out of me?", and "How can I lead in this conversation?" She feels an incredible surge of confidence and presence, fully aligned with her Mission. Nina decides to break free from the frantic cycle of daily posting and networking, and instead, she focuses on sharing only three purposeful and aligned posts per week. Her words resonate with her most perfect clients, who are magnetically drawn to her authentic message. Nina's reality begins to shift — she finds herself having sales calls only with ideal clients, who are abundant in number. Gone are the friction and pressure, replaced by a sense of spaciousness and unwavering certainty in her abilities.

***

By now, I trust you're starting to see that the old filter on your beliefs is created by conditioning, imprinting from childhood, social pressure, karmic trauma, and many other things, but ultimately it is determined by who you are BE-ing — your Identity.

Emotions don't happen to you, they can't be caught from other people — emotions are self-created and chemical. You can change your negative emotion ANY time (this is the real power of self-mastery!) but the key lies in doing it from the beginning of the broadcast chain, and not at the level of emotion.

And here's the best part — your identity is not set in stone. It is not an unchangeable fate that you are forever bound to. *You have the power to shape and redefine it according to your deepest desires.* This, my dear Leader, is the biggest secret of all. You are not limited to what you have been conditioned to believe. You can break free and become anything you desire, guided by the specific parameters you choose to embrace as your truth. The magic lies in realizing that you can be anything, absolutely anything your heart yearns for. And how does this divine transformation manifest in the material realm? Ah, it is intricately woven into the fabric of your Soul Design Strategy.

You've heard the phrase "we have free will" thrown around, but do you truly comprehend its significance? Well, let me illuminate its essence for you. "Free will" means we have the freedom to WILL ourselves into the very essence of who we ARE. It means that you possess the remarkable capacity to become whoever you decide to be. It is a choice, my dear, a sacred and resolute decision that you make with every fiber of your being.

But to truly be transformative, your decision must reverberate through every level of your broadcast. Just like it did for Emily and Nina — that is how it changes your identity — it must course through your veins, permeate your thoughts, and radiate from your very core. To manifest your chosen identity in the three-dimensional realm, you must fully embody it, not merely entertain it as a fleeting thought.

Now, my dear, embrace the truth of your power and let your decision echo through the cosmos. You are the alchemist of your own existence. It all begins by permanently shifting your broadcast, thereby forging a new identity that empowers you to manifest your Vision and become well-resourced for your Soul Mission.

Again, one of the things me and my team do for my clients is help you zero in on the root of your energetic broadcast issue. This takes years of experience, and we have *decades*. Go here to book a call to see how we can help you: eugeniaoganova.com/start .

In the upcoming Chapter 10, we'll look into incorporating the Seven Sacred Rules into your Future Identity. These principles are the bedrock of your Wealth by Soul Design — and they will enable you to step into the fullest expression of your divine essence.

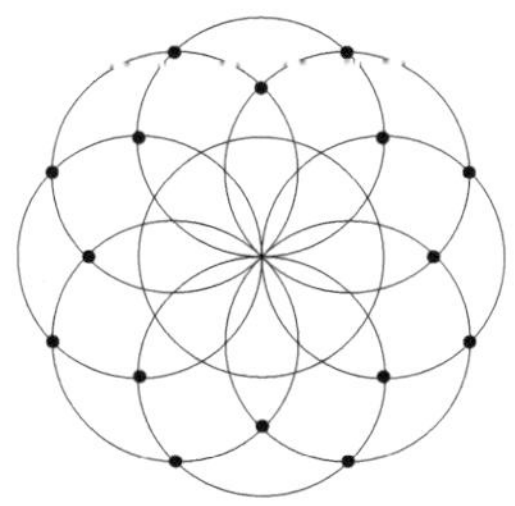

Chapter 10:

ACTIVATING INNER RULES

"You are what your deep, driving desire is. As your desire is, so is your will. As your will is, so is your deed. As your deed is, so is your destiny."

– SAGE YAJNAVALKYA, "BRIHADARANYAKA
UPANISHAD", 7TH CENTURY BC

Remember in Chapter 5 when we looked into the concept of Soul Discipline? And in Chapter 8, when we explored the Seven Sacred Rules in detail? These Rules serve as the pathway to your ultimate objective — an extraordinary and impactful 7-figure empire that catalyzes a shift in human consciousness.

Let me tell you, it's truly next-level to witness the Quantum leaps we are able to create when we embody the correct Future Identity, paired with a solid business strategy aligned to one's Soul Design. In just a matter of two to four months, my clients are making massive shifts and stepping fully into their power, achieving what most people might take years to attain. In fact, it's absolutely possible to make a Quantum leap into a 7-figure reality in less than two years — and I've seen it happen!

But let me be clear (the "fine print" from the Universe here): this requires an unwavering commitment and a ton of effort — both in terms of doing the inner work and implementing solid business strategies.

However, when we're aligned with our Soul Design Strategy, we can make leaps forward instead of inching our way there.

So let me remind you, beautiful Soul, that you've got to put in the work — but what kind of work matters — we want to be efficient, right? And when you do, the results will be extraordinary.

Just like my clients who embody their Future Identity, break through limiting beliefs, implement correct-for-them business strategy, and begin showing up as the successful, abundant entrepreneurs they were meant to be.

What is a miracle, really?

It's simply an occurrence that defies the laws of logic and physics — it's a cosmic wink from the Universe, reminding us that anything is possible. And here's the thing: you can predictably manifest these miracles in your business and life.

Now, it's time to assist you in integrating the Seven Sacred Rules, addressing your relationship with each one, and refining them to align with your Future Identity. Together, we will ensure their seamless implementation, propelling you towards your desired outcome.

The exercises below will take some time, you can do them now, or you can always come back to them when it's the right time for deep reflection.

My point here is — these are the exercises that will help your LIFE — so do them consistently to really get the value of becoming the identity of the Future You that has it all! You're worth it ;)

Rule #1: *Embrace the belief that it is already done.* Let's grab your journal and dive in.

❖ Take a moment to explore your beliefs about what is possible for you. What limitations have you placed on yourself and your business, and why?
❖ Then, envision what you truly desire to create in your business.
❖ Identify any factors within your control that sabotage your trust in your ability to manifest this desire.
❖ Who do you need to become in order to manifest all your desires? (List at least 3 qualities that are different from who you are now).
❖ Now, let's focus on practical ways to remind yourself that it is already done. Create a personalized reminder system that reinforces your Future Identity (incorporate a visual, a sound/ melody, a smell, an emotion, a body sensation).
❖ ·   Whenever you find yourself questioning how to achieve something, shift your perspective to embodying the Future Identity rather than seeking answers.

Remember, it's about embracing the certainty that your desires are **already manifested** and allowing your *actions* to align with this truth.

This is where you release the need to constantly "figure it out" and strive to get there, because it is already done.

If you find yourself desperately seeking the way, it means you are resisting actually BEING there — where it is already accomplished in the Quantum field.

It is always *already here.* You have the power to instantly shift into the new awareness where your desires already exist. Your success is inevitable. It is done. You can choose to wait, or you can swiftly call it in.

This is how embodying your Future Identity (based on this Rule #1) creates the balance between taking correct action and being in tune with the divine flow — so that you release the friction and leverage your uniqueness to manifest Wealth by Soul Design.

Rule #2: *Elevate your Risk Factor.* Let's dive into this empowering principle.

❖ What are the triggers that tend to evoke indecisiveness within you?

❖ What are you protecting? Explore the underlying reasons behind your hesitations.

❖ What familiar defense mechanisms do you employ to avoid making decisions that involve risk?

❖ Question the notion that risk is inherently negative. What else can risk be?

❖ What does your own risk factor mean to you?

❖ What does the version of yourself, who can make decisions swiftly and confidently, look like? Feel like? What sensations arise in this state of decisive action?

❖ What intentional steps must you take to maintain this state of powerful Future Identity? Cultivate self-trust? Practice making small decisions quickly? What else?

By embracing your risk factor and decisive action, you unleash your potential for successfully manifesting your Vision. *The speed and clarity of your decision-making is directly related to your perceived risk tolerance.* No one's Soul Design is to be indecisive! When you're in motion, it's easier for your energy guides to support you and guide you to shortcuts! But when you're standing still, waiting for the perfect solution to appear magically, you limit the assistance you can receive.

If you want to generate wealth you must lead, create value in the world. And that means — consistently increasing your risk-tolerance: stepping out of your comfort zone and embracing the unknown. Worrying about the potential risks and outcomes only drains your energy and distracts you from taking the right action in your business.

Your Soul Design and this Sacred Rule hold the key to your success, and by embodying it fully, you can become your Future You, eliminate friction, and effortlessly manifest your desired outcomes.

Rule #3: *Doubt is always a liar.* Let's dive into the depths of this powerful truth:

❖ What are your habitual doubts about yourself and your business?

❖ What if you decided that you are born worthy and destined for success, and thus never again have to prove yourself? How would this profound shift impact your business and its trajectory?

❖ Who would you be without the weight of doubt? (List at least 3 qualities that are different from who you are now).

❖ What if, from now on, you acknowledged doubt's presence without reacting or succumbing to its deceptive messages? How would your business be different if you simply observed doubt without allowing it to hinder your progress?

❖ What decision about your Identity do you have to make to never believe your doubt again?

❖ How awesome are you?

Embrace your awesomeness, dear Leader, and become unfuckwithable, for in this alignment, you are unfazed by external influences — NOTHING can touch you. You are truly free to co-create your future with the Universe.

Rule #4: *Do what it takes until it takes.* Time to unleash your unwavering commitment.

❖ On the scale of 1 (rarely) to 10 (always), how often do you follow through on your own business decisions despite the challenging circumstances, resistance, or emotional wobbles?

❖ What are your favorite tactics for sabotaging decisive action? How do thoughts like "I don't want to..." or "it just doesn't feel right" play a role in preventing you from taking the necessary steps in your business?

❖ What is the underlying story you tell yourself about why you can't or won't take action? What are you protecting through these habitual resistance stories?

❖ Who do you have to be in order to effortlessly follow through on all your aligned decisions without encountering friction? (Identify at least three qualities that you are currently not fully embodying).

❖ What if the next time you had to write a post, you simply sat your butt in the chair and didn't get up till it was done? What if reaching out to an event host or finalizing video materials for your offer became a seamless, friction-less non-eventful action? What if it always was a NON-event? What would it feel like?

❖ Which mindset shifts must you implement right now to align with the Future You who effortlessly takes the necessary actions without being entangled in resistance-based stories?

By fully embracing this rule, you liberate yourself from the illusion of external authority. No more rebelling against what truly serves your highest good. Soul Discipline, dear conscious Leader, is the mastery of making a decision and following through on it. Regardless of emotional reactions, negative thoughts, doubts, fears, or bodily sensations. You take the emotion out of action (you can always have a moment to process that emotion later, after the action is done!)

Rule #5: *Become an Observer of Truth.* Let's awaken your ability to perceive reality of Soul Truth.

- ❖ Rate yourself on the scale of 1 (rarely) to 10 (always) on how often are you able to observe events in your business without being consumed by the unnecessary drama? (Examples of drama include your own crazy thoughts and worries that blow things out of proportion, client drama that you take on as your own, money drama, hiring drama, and so on).
- ❖ What habitual worry resides in your body? Is it a sense of being too much or too little, too similar or too different, too structured or too flexible? Or a worry that you can't make something happen, won't figure it out, will disappoint someone? What else?
- ❖ Are you able to locate a higher perspective in any situation despite personal emotional reactions? Can you observe and comprehend the lessons embedded within your emotional responses, thoughts, and inactions?
- ❖ Are you willing to eliminate seductive drama in your business and marketing? What happens when you perceive the purity of your experiences without getting entangled in unnecessary drama? How does it transform your business?
- ❖ Who do you need to be in order to gain perspective? Identify at least three qualities that you currently lack.
- ❖ What must you change in your mindset and approach to business and marketing in order to never get caught in the drama again?

When you become the Observer, the truth becomes obvious amidst the noise of lies. You can see your lessons, identify solutions, and know exactly what to say to your potential clients. Guiding your clients through the sales process becomes second nature. You navigate team dynamics with ease. You remain anchored in your authentic truth despite any crunchy money situations that might arise, transcending the conditioned lies that accompany the human experience.

Rule #6: *I always get what I came for.* Let's explore this rule in depth:

- What does your business landscape look like currently?
- Where are the places you feel you didn't get what you wanted or expected? This could include courses you purchased, coaches you joined, or clients who didn't achieve desired results. What else?
- In these situations, where have you placed responsibility for your fulfillment or results? Onto these external factors such as that course, that coach, that client? Why do you resist taking ownership of your outcomes?
- Do you trust that the Universe always delivers, even if you don't immediately see the value in what is being delivered?
- Who do you need to be in order to consistently receive what you've decided you will get, or something even better? Identify at least three qualities that you currently lack.
- What changes must you implement in your mindset to approach your personal development, your business, marketing, your clients — with the expectations that they will deliver on their roles?

If you're not receiving what you desire, it is feedback from the Universe to recalibrate your expectations and focus. Rule #6 is about expecting others to show up and fulfill their roles.

Your needs will always be met. Being Soul-led and aligning with your unique Soul Design attracts what is in harmony with your purpose. And let me remind you, every Soul Design includes access to Wealth!

When you consistently channel your energy through expectation and embody your Future Identity, you broadcast your intentions at the frequency of Quantum Wealth, making manifestation inevitable.

Rule #7: *I am always abundant.*
- ❖ Why are you NOT at multi-6 or 7-figures right now? How do you sabotage your abundance?
- ❖ What are the most common stories you tell yourself about your limitations and scarcity?
- ❖ What are the 3 top reasons you believe abundance is available for everyone else but you? (I know, a tricky question, but just ask your Lower Self and she'll tell you)
- ❖ What are the daily thoughts of the Future You? The one who already arrived at that level of "booked with dream high-ticket clients", "amazing $100k launch", "featured speaker at the top event in your industry"?
- ❖ What are the daily actions the Future You takes to grow and scale her 7-figure empire? How does this differ from what you are doing now?
- ❖ What must change today for abundance in your life to be as natural as breathing?

By understanding the law of Quantum Entanglement (from Chapter 8), you realize that what you deeply desire already exists in the Quantum field, eagerly awaiting your arrival. Abundance is the fundamental nature of the Universe, and the notion of "lack" is merely a human-created illusion.

The miracles and extraordinary manifestations you seek are not distant dreams but an inherent part of your divine birthright. As you immerse yourself in limitless possibilities, you bear witness to the *supernatural* unfolding in your reality. Unleash your inherent power, dance to the rhythm of your Soul, and create a reality that radiates true wealth. This is the manifestation of your unique Wealth by Soul Design.

***

By taking the time to complete each set of questions for each of the Rules, you come closer to being able to manifest your desired future — because the more you play with these Rules and embody them (clearing what's in the way) the more you become YOU who is already there, waiting for you to finally catch up!

Your Soul Design Strategy begins here, embodying the Sacred Rules that are the pathway to the frictionless business of multi-6 or 7-figures. This is how you create your empire, dear Leader!

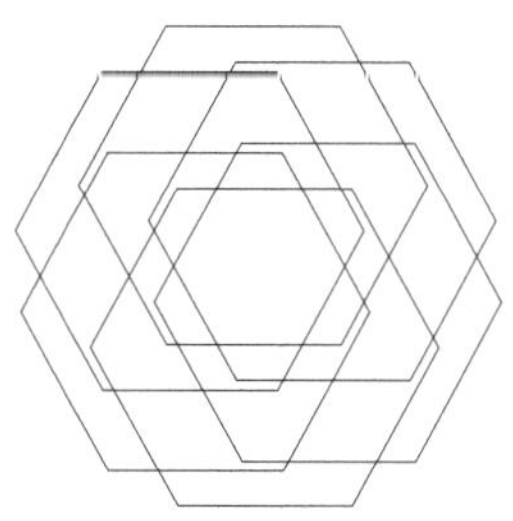

Conclusion: Creating Your Soul-Led Empire

Dear Leader — Wow! You've made it to the end of this epic book (or should I say *Journey?*), and let me tell you, I am beyond freaking proud of you! You've shown up like the magical badass you are, taking your business and yourself seriously. And guess what? You've learned so much along the way — why you've felt stuck, overwhelmed, and unable to scale.

And now, my friend, it's time to recap our journey and celebrate your growth.

❖ The first few chapters of this book were all about taking a deep dive into the current state of your business. We boldly explored your niche, message, and sales clarity. We fearlessly faced the areas that needed some serious improvement and handed you the golden ticket of possible actions to take based on your assessments. Boom! Now **you've got a clear-as-day picture of where you can level up** like a lightning bolt — and **how the Soul Design Strategy is going to solve all your damn challenges!**

- ❖ Then, the game got real as we unleashed the power of *understanding and implementing* **your Soul Design Strategy.** It should be clear to you by now how it is **the key component to sustainably scaling your business in a Soul-led way,** without forcing yourself into cookie-cutter strategies, masculine sales, or pressuring yourself to do what is unnatural to you. We dove headfirst into what un-aligned marketing looks like — and the price you pay for it. You were also introduced to **your Archetypes and the concept of Soul Discipline as the way to allow you to implement the correct strategy and scale into multi-6 or 7-figures without friction.**

- ❖ In the next big chapter of the book, we explored The Conscious F.U.T.U.R.E. Method itself. No more playing small or chasing after trendy tactics that only leave you feeling tricked or defeated — you now have the way to sustainably grow your business. We dove into the **solid linear strategies like market positioning, premium offers, messaging, lead generation, sales, and scaling of your business. We made sure to align it all to your Soul Expertise and unique Archetypes. By the end, you learned how your unique superpowers can be woven into all the aspects of the Method — and how you can leverage your uniqueness to turn your Soul Design into the Wealth you deserve.**

- ❖ Then, we dove into the non-linear Quantum creation — that's where the real magic unfolded. We **tapped into the power of the Future Identity, pulling in the most lucrative timelines from the Quantum field.** We focused on the Seven Sacred Rules to guide you in taking inspired action without any of that soul-sucking pressure. We investigated the practical ways to elevate your frequency so you can show up as the unique Leader of human evolution while **unapologetically manifesting boundless Wealth.**

Now, my magical badass Leader, it's time for the next step.

It's simple, but it's oh-so-freaking-important.

Are you ready?

Commit. And then DO it.

Commit like you've never committed before.

Implement everything you've learned and elevate your frequency in every single freaking *moment*. From this moment forward, you are all in!

Decide if you want some help on this wild journey *(I'm always here to support you!)*,

or if you wanna bootstrap it again, going it alone.

But whatever you choose, make that decision *quick*.

It's not about becoming an overnight millionaire. It's about embracing your unique Soul Design Strategy and watching it unfold over time. It's about cranking up your frequency like a rockstar and receiving the flow of wealth while serving at the level higher than you've ever dreamed of.

And it all starts with *your aligned action.*

You are destined for greatness. You're here to activate mind-blowing healing, ignite passion in marriages, heal broken hearts, download methods that skyrocket abundance flow, and liberate humanity from the chains of ancestral karmic BS. You are a force to be reckoned with — a special, unique, and unfuckwithable Leader.

You are meant to be well-resourced for doing your Soul Work in the world — it's the Universal Law of Service.

But let's get real for a moment.

Most people out there, despite having the freaking seeds of brilliance within them, do nothing. They let their potential wither away like a sad little houseplant.

But not you, my friend. You're different.

You've got that fire burning deep within your Soul, and you're ready to unleash it upon the world.

Listen up, because this is important.

It takes magical badass unicorns like us to change the world. We do things our way, on our terms, and guess what? We actually DO change the world! And we're meant to get paid damn well for it.

That's right — you're not here to play small. You're here to make a massive impact, create a freaking revolution in human consciousness (God knows, humanity needs you!), and fill your bank accounts with overflowing abundance. You're unstoppable!

If you're **feeling the call to get support** on this epic journey, reach out to us and let's have a conversation: eugeniaoganova.com/start .

We're ready to rock and roll with you!

We're really good at what we do — just like you're a master at your unique craft. If you possess those unique superpowers that the world so desperately needs, we want to be the ones who help you unleash them like a hurricane of awesomeness.

So, dear Leader, as we conclude the "first chapter" of mind-blowing adventure together, perhaps we will write the next one together?

Either way, I want you to remember this:

If you leverage your unique badass inner magic through aligned actions....

Your success is inevitable.

Your power is unmatched.

And your impact will shake the very foundations of this world and uplevel human consciousness.

You manifest Wealth by Soul Design.

To your continued badassery and Soul-led success!

- Eugenia Oganova

About the Author

Eugenia Oganova is an international Business Soul Strategist, Marketing Energetics Coach, and Transcension Mentor with 20 years of experience.

She has been featured in over 100 networks and publications and is a self-made millionaire.

Eugenia specializes in helping female Coaches & Healers leverage their uniqueness to sustainably scale into multi-6 and 7-figures.

Her process helps them add $10k-$50k per month without forcing themselves to work harder — by aligning their Business with their unique Soul Design Strategy.

Eugenia is the creator of the Conscious F.U.T.U.R.E. Method that unites "masculine/linear" Business Strategy with "feminine/non-linear" Quantum Energetics, so coaches can attract ideal clients who happily pay premium prices instead of chasing after them.

Her methodology empowers coaches to elevate into their Future identity and create custom high-ticket business, without burning out or sacrificing their needs.

Eugenia is a best-selling author of 3 books: "Mission Alpha — The Wise and Passionate You", "Awakening the Harmony Within — How to Create with Spirit", and "The Secret of Sekhmet — Why Akhenaten Challenged the Gods of Egypt".

Not a typical business coach or writer: Eugenia is clairvoyant and neurodivergent, and she uses her extraordinary abilities to support her clients in addition to solid business strategies.

Check out Eugenia's services and paid and free courses at www.EugeniaOganova.com

- ❖ If you are at the beginning stages of your business — Eugenia can help you untangle your message and infuse your business with marketing strategies that feel natural so you can finally get paid well for your Soul Work.
- ❖ If you're a seasoned busy coach ready to scale — Eugenia is here to fine-tune your market-positioning, refine your message, and streamline your offers and operations, setting you on a trajectory towards 7-figures and beyond in a Soul-led way.

Reach out at eugeniaoganova.com/start

Made in United States
Orlando, FL
05 March 2024